COMMUNITY, CHURCH
AND HEALING

COMMUNITY, CHURCH and HEALING

A study of some of the corporate aspects of the Church's Ministry to the sick

R. A. LAMBOURNE,
B.D., M.B., Ch.B., D.P.M.

DARTON, LONGMAN & TODD
LONDON

DARTON, LONGMAN & TODD LTD.
64 CHISWICK HIGH ROAD
LONDON, W.4

Printed in Great Britain by Jarrold & Sons Ltd, Norwich

CONTENTS

PREFACE

RECENT YEARS HAVE SEEN a revival of interest within Medicine and Church in the possibility of co-operation with each other. There is now, amongst the majority of men and women working in the medical and social services, some sympathy with church and religion. This is something new, for before two world wars shook man's confidence in his ability to master the world and himself, a mood of atheism or condescending agnosticism was dominant in Medicine. One sign of these new times is that universities and hospitals founded at the end of last century without a chapel are now building chapels and appointing chaplains. Another is the growing emphasis amongst doctors upon a holistic approach to medicine. This holistic approach respects the fact of the psychosomatic unity of the person. As a consequence the clinician, whatever his personal position in matters of faith, now recognises that ideally no case history is complete which does not record some understanding of the patient's thoughts and feelings about his place and purpose in the universe. This understanding is not, of course, necessarily communicated in religious language.

The Church, stimulated by this more sympathetic attitude of Medicine and by the enthusiasm of a few of its own clergy and many health practitioners from Christian Science and similar religious bodies on the fringe of Christian practice, is taking more seriously its ministry to the sick. However, perhaps because of the backgrounds of these enthusiasts, the theology of the movement has been sparse and often unsound. With no call for lecturers on the subject in university, theological college, or post-ordination college, there has been a not surprising lack of academic research on medico-pastoral theology, and our library shelves illustrate this defect.

In this situation any attempt at serious theological discussion may be helpful. For this book the mode of discussion has been

dictated by what I believe to be the most evident weaknesses
of prevalent medico-pastoral theology, and by present theological interest in the Church today. The former I believe
to be its gnosticism and individualism. The latter we take to be
incarnational theology and the liturgical revival with its strong
corporate emphasis. Happily these two theological concerns are
matched by two recent trends of Medicine. Firstly it is coming
to feel itself at home, and only fully at home, within the wider
discipline of human biology. Secondly it is being increasingly
affected by the younger disciplines of sociology and anthropology. Thus it is that for theology, sin, and for medicine,
sickness, is now recognised to be something that must be studied,
understood, and remedied within the body corporate.

In this book I first explore the hypothesis, that sin and sickness are symptoms of communal disorder, are experienced by the
community, and yield to therapeutic measures designed to
improve the community considered as an organic whole. Then,
turning to the Bible, I argue that the Old Testament is in part
the record of how obedience of the People of God made for unity
and wholeness whilst disobedience lead towards divisions and
sickness. I then show that for the New Testament authors
Christ's healing ministry largely consisted of public dramas in
which the participant observers responded to a crisis, moving
themselves either towards wholeness or towards disease. It is
then argued that the local church must remember and re-
capitulate these public healing work of Christ by acts of mercy
and healing done to the sick and suffering in its neighbourhood, and thereby make Christ 'really present' in the community. 'Really present,' because we must take seriously Christ's
real humanity in his healing ministry, and also his definite
assurances of his presence when mercy and healing is done
in his name. Therefore, it is reasoned that within the local
church's ministry to the sick the ordinary deed of mercy and
healing such as changing a wet bed, running to the chemist
for medicine, injecting penicillin, or making intercessory
prayer, becomes an occasion of grace—a true sacrament. And
in this sacrament, as in all of Christ's sacraments, community is created and the church becomes what it is—a
therapeutic community. The conclusion is that for the local

church a careful assessment of the needs of the neighbourhood, and a plan for their amelioration which includes an imaginative correlation of secular administration, practical measures, prayer, witness and sacrament is no optional extra but is the very ground of that church's being.

This book was conceived and executed whilst I was working in general medical practice. Dragged out of bed in the middle of the night with nothing but resentment in my heart, it happened that on several occasions I rebuked my disinclination to give proper attention to some unattractive person and to make a thorough examination. I rebuked myself with the remembrance of Christ's word 'Ye did it unto me', and then it suddenly seemed that Christ was really and literally present under my hands in the form of the sick person. I saw him and I touched him. That experience in a life troubled by frequent doubts and many failings inspired the incarnational and sacramental theology of this book. The other dominant theme, the corporate one, I also owe to general practice, for there I saw how family and neighbourhood disorder would over the years manifest itself by symptoms in one of its members after another.

My first acknowledgements must therefore be to my patients and their friends and neighbours. When, perplexed by my experiences, I turned to the Theology Department of the University of Birmingham and became a student again, I had help and understanding from all the staff. To the Reverend Professor G. W. H. Lampe and the Reverend Professor J. G. Davies, successively heads of that Department, I am especially indebted, for they guided my studies and supervised the preparation of the B.D. thesis upon which this book is based. Without my friend the Reverend David Paton's continuing encouragement I could never have finished this work, and his reading of the proofs was just one more of many acts of friendship. I thank Messrs. Darton, Longman & Todd for their confidence in accepting this book and for the courtesies shown me during its preparation for publication. Much of chapter 7 appeared in an article in *Theology* and much of chapter 11 in *Frontier*, and I thank the proprietors of these periodicals for permission to reproduce this material. Finally I thank my wife who shared with me the physical and mental fatigue which the writing of a book in the midst of a full family and professional life entails, and who suffered with me the many long periods of despression and doubt which threatened its survival.

CHAPTER 1

THE LOCAL COMMUNITY AND THE PRESENT MEDICAL SITUATION

I F THE AVERAGE MAN in the street were asked to describe the various services which aid the sick, he would enumerate the different components of what we usually call The National Health Service: the work done by the hospitals, by general practitioners, and by the Local Authority. This opinion would in all probability be shared by many medical practitioners, and indeed appear to be so obvious as to make the question seem stupid. To the modern mind, treatment of the sick suggests hospitals, doctors, ambulances, syringes, white coats, X-rays, drugs, nurses, Executive Councils, and a host of other special things.

When we enquire more deeply into the matter, however, it is not quite as it seems. We are being misled by a modern emphasis on one particular aspect of caring for the sick. It was not always so. Until this century most people in this country received help in their sickness from only their own family and neighbours. Some of these helpers, of course, had special experience, as in herbal remedies or childbirth, but by and large the sick child, man, or woman received his care in the home, and from his family and neighbours.

It is not necessary to emphasise that the state of affairs just described was accompanied by disastrous morbidity and mortality rates, and that the provision of trained medical attention and of a suitable environment, often away from home, was a most urgent task. Nothing in this book is intended to imply that there is necessarily any special virtue in voluntary or unqualified aid to the sick, which renders it superior to or more spiritual than specialised medical service. The building up of a vast hospital and specialist service over the last hundred years was the only answer to a situation in which the majority of men and women could not get adequate medical or domestic care in the vast conglomerations of over-crowded houses thrown up by the Industrial Revolution. But it is necessary that we emphasise that what we tend to regard as normative in the way of medical services is, in fact, a particular answer to a particular situation, and that therefore it may need to change with the times.

There is, in fact, beneath the Health Service as we know it, and as we usually think of it, with hospitals, specialists, general practitioners, and public health services, a vaster health service with an army of workers. These are the mothers, fathers, brothers, sisters, sons and daughters, and other relatives and neighbours of sick men and women who care for them, and it is they who carry the major burden of caring for the sick in terms of man-hours and domestic arts, if not in terms of trained skill. This statement seems improbable at first sight, but a rough measurement of the hours of sickness the average man or woman spends in bed at home would soon support it. How many hospitals would be needed if mothers did not nurse their children through the common infectious illnesses, if husbands did not help to care for their wives after childbirth or during influenza, and if daughters and neighbours did not clean, shop, cook for and nurse the elderly? The truth is that the care for the sick is like an iceberg. Visible is the National Health Service which we have in our mind's eye, but invisible is a much vaster service in the hands of relatives and neighbours. It is fatal to forget this truth, for the size and nature of what is visible is being determined, in part, by what is beneath.

What has been said above may appear to be so obvious that it has not been worth saying: but, as is so often true, the obvious is frequently overlooked. The centre of gravity of medical education, imagination, research, and influence during the past fifty years has been the general hospital, full of individual patients in bed and well insulated from family and community. Increasing specialisation has made matters worse, so that it has not been easy to consider the patient as a whole person, let alone one who normally moves and has his being in a community. It would not be unfair to say that twenty years ago in the medical schools there was a grave lack of appreciation of the social aspects of disease. Public Health studies were included in the curriculum, but they were largely concerned with control of epidemics of the common infectious diseases, and the student was required to know little beyond the first principles of safe sewage disposal, provision of pure food and water supplies, and methods of isolation of infectious patients. This situation was no doubt largely due to the fact that the previous decades had been absorbed in the vital task of controlling killing epidemic diseases, like diphtheria and typhoid fever, and acute surgical and medical conditions such as appendicitis and pneumonia. But, as is so often the case in all organisations, including professional ones, there is a time-lag between the emergence of fresh needs and the adaptation of old procedures. So in medicine there is a hiatus between new concepts of disease and the reformation of existing medical education and organised medical services.

The neglect of the social origins of disease was, of course, never complete. There was an attempt to deal with social origins in two spheres in particular, industrial medicine and maternity and child care, and great strides were made. In industry, hazards in factories were controlled by legislation; in maternity and child welfare, the emphasis upon education of the mother was the first modern medical effort on a large scale to influence the *personal* environment of the person at risk to sickness. It was realised that the morbidity and mortality rates of babies and infants and children were influenced as much by the quality of care provided by the mother as by the medical services and knowledge available. Here is a clear case of the iceberg. Beneath the visible mass of the medical services given to babies in general practitioners' surgeries, out-patient clinics, and in-patient services, was a greater but invisible mass of paediatric care in countless homes. It was the 'medical services' available to infants at home, and given by the mothers of the country, which determined the shape and size of the specialised services required by children. The education of mothers in welfare clinics was the means of changing the 'local community medical services' given at home, and thus the shape of the national health services required. If mothers were the same today as fifty years ago we should need many more doctors, nurses, hospitals, and all that goes to provide a paediatric service.

The general practitioner is often described as the essential ground base of the National Health Service and there is great truth in this, for he is the first step in the ladder of organised services, the first of these to diagnose and treat: but long before him in the natural history of health and disease is the part played by the patient himself and his community, whether that community be a root family group or a larger house community, street, or neighbourhood group. It is here that the National Health Service is based, here that the first diagnosis and treatment is given, so that just as the quality of general practitioner service is vital to the National Health Service, so is the quality of 'local community medical service' even more vital. The deficiencies, avoidable or unavoidable, of the general practitioner service, whatever their causes, have to be met from other directions such as from Local Authority clinics or hospital out-patients. Every area of medical service not covered by the general practitioner is an area of medical service that has to be taken over by someone else. Similarly, each failure, avoidable or unavoidable, of the natural local group in house and street to act as early diagnosers, home helps, good mothers, hygienic food providers, wet bed changers, absorbers of neurotic and psychotic behaviour, and in many other ways, means an area of medical service surrendered which has to be covered by someone else.

The education of the mother in order to raise her efficiency in playing her natural part as the the giver of a medical service has already been mentioned. It is not surprising that in the mother-child relationship we should see the prototype of the medical service given in the local community, for the total dependence of the baby upon his mother, and the normal deep sense of responsibility to the child felt by the mother, makes deficiencies in this medical service very apparent when they occur. Similarly, we shall find that when the dependence of the baby is mirrored in other sickness situations the efficiency of the 'local community medical service' in house and home becomes a vital matter to the National Health Service. The second childhood of old age receives its medical service, like the baby, normally from its natural root group of the family supported by friends and neighbours. Wherever this local medical service fails, not necessarily through the fault of its members, there is a new area of responsibility for the Local Authority or National Health Service. What is true of the total dependence of childhood and second childhood is true in lesser degree of many other medical situations.

We are becoming accustomed to articles in the medical Press pointing out the large proportion of patients occupying hospital beds for what are described as social reasons, most especially in the case of maternity services and services for the aged and the mentally sick. These social reasons are not merely an index of monetary poverty, but of poverty of 'local community medical service' in all its aspects, available in the house and neighbourhood. Old age, infirmity, three pounds a week, a good daughter living round the corner, and you may stay at home. Old age, infirmity, and even six pounds a week and no one round the corner, and you may go to hospital. Thus Townsend summarises his observations of the population of an East London geriatric hospital by saying:[1]

> The conclusion is that those admitted to a local geriatric hospital differed markedly from the general population of old people in their family and social circumstances. Apart from differences in marital status, which broadly confirm previous findings, there were three significant features of the family circumstances of those in hospital: (1) The unmarried and the childless formed 43 per cent of the people in hospital, compared with 18 per cent of people in Bethnal Green. (2) Only 39 per cent of those in hospital had surviving daughters compared with 71 per cent outside. (3) A higher proportion of those in hospital had been geographically isolated from children when living at home. These conclusions apply only to one hospital for the chronic sick and require confirmation elsewhere, but on this showing marriage and the availability of children, particularly of daughters, is a strong protection against admission to hospital.

It may be objected that the use of the words 'local community medical service' to describe the untrained services given by family, friends, and neighbours in the home is unfortunate, because it blurs the distinction between welfare services and

---

[1] P. Townsend, *Family Life of Old People*, Routledge and Kegan Paul, 1957, p. 187

'real' medical services. But because we are concerned to show
how health and disease are a response to the totality of man's
experience, it seems better to err in this manner than contribute
to compartmentalism. After all it is the same person who is fed
and X-rayed, clothed and injected, loved and incised, sheltered
and dosed. The same Health Visitor gives advice on inocula-
tions and housewifery, the same general practitioner gives
advice on influenza and diet, the same surgeon gives advice on
rupture and heavy lifting, the same physician advice on asthma
and living with mother-in-law. Side by side in the same
maternity unit lie women admitted because they need hospital
equipment and hospital staff at hand to ensure a safe delivery,
and others who would be better confined at home, if home were
satisfactory. A satisfactory home means not only bricks and
mortar, but someone to be mother's help as well. Side by side
in the same geriatric unit lie elderly people in need of special
skills and equipment provided at great expense, and others with
ailments better treated at home if only a satisfactory home were
available, and 'a satisfactory home' includes relatives, friends,
and neighbours who can lend a hand.

From what has been said so far it might be thought that it is
implied that there is no attempt in this country to give due
emphasis to the study of the social pathology of disease and to
legislation and reorganisation of the National Health Service.
This is not intended. In many quarters there is an increasing
stress on this subject, and general medicine is turning gradually,
though sometimes with some suspicion, to the social sciences to
form a partnership both for research and for action within the
disciplines of medical services.

Giving his Presidential Address to the British Medical
Association at their Annual Meeting in 1958 Professor A. P.
Thomson, said:[1] 'In the curricula of most medical schools little
attention is given to the functions of medicine in relation to
society. The dramatic success of scientific methods in the treatment of individuals appeals to the young, and in teaching
hospitals absorbs their attention so exclusively that they tend to
ignore that large part of clinical practice which is not measur-
able in terms of science and which often has no relation to

[1] *British Medical Journal*, 19 July 1958.

organic disease.' And again later in the same address, speaking of the College of General Practitioners: 'I suggest to members of that College that they should consider an approach to university departments of social science to examine the techniques that have been developed for the study of human behaviour and the methods for recording information in forms suitable for analysis and in the hope that co-ordinated research may be established.' Later Professor Thomson quotes with approval Canon C. E. Raven: 'I should like to see the province of medicine extended; I should like to see certain departments of the great profession equipped to study diseases of the corporate life. I believe that there is room here for the application of precisely the same skills in diagnosis and treatment which the social worker does not have and which the medical man does. I am not depreciating the work of the social worker at all. But I am suggesting that between sociology and medicine there might be established the same co-operation as between psychology and medicine.'[1]

Such work as Professor Thomson suggests has become increasingly common of recent years, and particular attention has been given to the social factors which determine whether the elderly infirm and sick can remain in the community or must be admitted to hospital or old person's home. The capacity of the elderly infirm and sick to manage by themselves or with the help of relatives has been shown to be large. One survey[2] showed over 1 per cent of old age pensioners bedridden at home and over 7 per cent confined to the house. In a population containing 7,000,000 old age pensioners this means 70,000 bedridden and 490,000 confined to the house. With such large numbers, even a small change for the worse in community care must mean a flood of patients to the hospitals. These hospitals are already full to bursting-point and much of their facilities are being squandered on patients who have been admitted for social rather than medical reasons, and who are 'needing none of the facilities traditionally associated with hospitals'.[3]

These various surveys have shown that it is the old people themselves and their relatives who provide the major part of the

1 *New Scientist*, 5 June 1958.
2 Hobson and Pemberton, *B.M.J.*, 1956, 1, 587.
3 Garratt, F. N., Lowe, C. R. and McKeown, T., *Lancet*, 1958b, 1.682.

health services to the old, and that the primary objective of the professional health services should be to support them in this task and to take over when the burden is too heavy. For, as a leading authority writes, 'there is no hope of carrying the burden of old age that the future has in store without assistance from the family and neighbours at least equal to that given at the present time'.[1]

The finding of a creative solution to the problems imposed by an increasing proportion of elderly people with unused abilities and unsatisfied needs is one of the great adventures of the age in which we live. Some recent sociological studies suggest that men and women are adapting themselves to the new situation with reasonable ingenuity and courage. The general picture is encouraging, and there seems to be little support for those pessimists who affirm that men and women no longer care for their families generally, and their parents in particular. Thus, for example, Willmott and Young[2] write: 'There are, of course, stress and worries for both young and old, the parents in particular often have to sacrifice their independence for companionship and care. But the fact remains that, in ill-health, infirmity or widowhood, the aged people are, by and large cared for by their children.' However, it is equally clear that the rapid changes of today throw great demands upon men and women in every neighbourhood, and especially new municipal housing estates, to re-establish the extended family from year to year in a pattern suitable for modern conditions. It is also clear that where geographical dispersal of old extended families is large and rapid the suffering in loneliness, mental strain, and nursing deprivation may be quite sharp. Moreover, success in maintaining or re-establishing such extended family networks is always threatened by the divisions which separate men and women. Some of these seem trivial as isolated issues, like dress, eating habits, spending habits, education preferences, car status, and sport selection, but together they are formidable obstacles. Because of such obstacles, geographical proximity and mutual need may not be strong enough to bring people together, and

[1] Sheldon, J. H., *B.M.J.*, 1950, 1.319.
[2] Willmott and Young, *Family and Class in a London Suburb*, Routledge and Kegan Paul, 1960, p. 57. See also Chalke, H. D. and Benjamin, B., 'The Aged in their own Homes', *Lancet*, 21 March 1953.

men and women may be deprived of company and neighbourly aid essential to their health. The strong blood ties of districts such as Bethnal Green[1] are often bought in part at the cost of a reduction in neighbourliness outside the kith and kin. Common class bonds in a road may leave isolated a family who have recently moved in, but who, socially speaking have not yet 'arrived'. Strong family ties in the children's family, and especially the egalitarian pattern of husband-wife relationships today, may cause psychic isolation of a parent, so that one of the commonest social complaints of older people living within the households of children is the feeling of isolation within the family group.[2]

Occupational mobility, which takes a third of sons up or down,[3] out of their father's class, has a demonstrable effect on social visiting in general and care of the aged in particular.

The question naturally arises as to what part the Churches play in these matters. Little is known. It is probable that they follow very much the influence of other community organisations in the broad effect they have upon the catalysis and inhibition of extended family networks. That is, they provide a meeting-ground in which friendships are made and sustained; but these friendships tend to be class structured. Thus R. H. T. Thompson, following his studies of four Birmingham parishes, was compelled to write:[4]

'The appeal of the Church rests on social compatibility rather than doctrinal conviction.

'As a result of the lack of distinctive ideology and a fellowship which overrode other considerations, the life of the parish church tended to reflect the divisions of society rather than reconcile and heal them.'

However, this cannot be the whole story. Experienced ministers would claim, probably with some justice, that a few Christians consistently endeavour to go 'the extra mile' and break some personal or social custom to make a friendship or do a merciful deed, and that most Christians do it occasionally,

---

[1] Cf. Willmott and Young, *Family and Kinship in East London*, Routledge and Kegan Paul, 1957.
[2] Kutner, B., *et al.*, *Five Hundred Over Sixty*, p. 110.
[3] Glass, D. V., *Social Mobility in Britain*, Routledge and Kegan Paul, 1951.
[4] *The Church's Understanding of Itself*, S.C.M. Press, 1957.

though far too seldom. There is a pressing need here for the
Church to employ sociologists so that every parish church can
be guided to look within its own boundaries and see what
actually is going on. The Church could then answer an allega-
tion such as that of Hazell[1] who writes: 'Yet, today, despite the
numerous churches in this country and the large number of
clergy of all denominations, no special emphasis has been made
by them of the duties of the family towards each other. It also
seems particularly unfortunate that whatever influence they
may have does not bear directly on the making of laws in
Britain.' Though this indictment may be unjust, the fact that it
is made is significant. Exhortations to neighbourliness are
frequent enough, and many Christians respond as individuals,
but parish assessment of its problems and parish planning to
deal with them are rare indeed.[2]

Some of the recent research into the care of the aged is
sufficient to demonstrate to what extent the health of the
individual is dependent upon the willingness and the ability
of the local community in home and street to share one another's
burdens. Thus, through the hard facts of everyday life, through
mundane matters of shopping, cooking, bed-pans, steep stairs,
soiled linen, vertigo, and fear of crossing the road alone, we are
'many members, yet but one body' (1 Cor. 12:20). From the
point of view of the sociologist the Churches, regarded merely
as secular phenomena, may be taken seriously as one of many
popular activities which raise the frequency and the 'depth' of
inter-personal contacts. If an agnostic sociologist estimates that
the effect of the Churches is to increase the amount of community responsibility to the sick, by fostering 'local community',
he may regard the Churches as healing forces. This indeed is
probably the view of many non-Christian sociologists who have
no use for the Gospel. It is strange to think that in this respect
the non-believer is more ready to see the healing work of the
Church as embodied in these mundane activities than many
Christians who search desperately for Christ's healing activity

---

[1] Hazell, K., *Social and Medical Problems of the Elderly*, Hutchinson, 1960, p. 194.
[2] M. Argyle's *Religious Behaviour*, Routledge and Kegan Paul, 1958, is an exception. For the possibilities of religious sociology, see Boulard's *An Introduction to
Religious Sociology*, trans. M. J. Jackson. Darton, Longman and Todd, 1961. See
also *The Family in Contemporary Society*, S.P.C.K., 1958.

in his Church today. Indeed they have eyes and see not, because they are looking only for a 'spiritual' healing, which they recognise as such only if it appears to operate by a 'non-physical' method, or if it is not available to non-Christian healers, or both. These grave theological distortions will be considered later. Here it seems sufficient to state that if the *only* mode of operation of the Church in bringing healing to the sick were by good deeds of nursing and housekeeping it could be claimed as a real work of Christ. It is to those who saw to the hungry, the thirsty, the cold, the sick, the homeless, and the imprisoned that at the Last Day the Son says 'Come, ye blessed of my Father, inherit the kingdom prepared . . . from the foundation of the world' (Matt. 25:34). However, it is not *only* through the soma but through the psyche that the local community heals the sick. We must now turn to the subject of mental health, where this fact is well demonstrated.

CHAPTER 2

MENTAL HEALTH AND THE
LOCAL COMMUNITY

IT HAS ALREADY BEEN stated that there is a growing recognition in medicine that the social pathology of disease makes every aspect of community life relevant to the prevention and treatment of disease in the individual. In particular, the dependence of the baby upon the mother for its survival was mentioned as epitomising this fact of mutual dependence in the field of health. The problem of maintaining the aged in health, and preserving them when in sickness has already been considered, but it is in psychiatry that this concept of the corporate life as the groundwork for health has been most developed in theory and practice. The consequence is a complete change in the attitude towards the mentally sick, which is leading to a revision of the view which regarded a hospital as a place where medical people 'do something' to the sick individuals detained in the building. The extent of this 'new look' is indicated by the growing number of articles in medical journals on the organisation of hospitals as a community. J. R. Rees,[1] Director of the World Federation of Mental Health, after speaking optimistically of the possibilities for cure of mental illness by physical methods, goes on to say 'None the less . . . in the good hospitals there is much evidence that the general atmosphere, the interest in, and respect for patients which are displayed, are possibly more important for the majority of patients than are the physical methods of treatment.'

We have running through the whole world of psychiatry today a stress on the importance of personal relationships as a factor in the prevention and cure of mental illness. This stress is partly a rediscovery of an old and obvious fact, a rediscovery which all Western civilisation had to make after the excessive individualism of the last century. It is also the result of new

[1] In *American Journal of Psychiatry*, December 1958.

knowledge from the fields of sociology, anthropology, and group psychotherapy. There is new information, and new technical language to classify this information, about the social behaviour of animals and humans. Thus it is that even in individual psychoanalysis the emphasis is no longer on identifying the infantile primitive forces which power the present behaviour of the patient, and on bringing this knowledge to the patient that he may appropriate it, and thus receive the benefits. The emphasis is rather on the interpretation in terms of infantile 'phantasy' of what is going on 'here and now' between analyst and analysand, that is, a study of the 'transference' and 'counter-transference'. It is by an act of will to analyse what the group of two (analyst and analysand) are doing to each other in the interest of inner personal distortions of the truth, that healing comes. That is, the quality of health of the group of two in the individual analysis is dependent on the quality of their 'I—Thou'[1] relationship 'here and now'. The analysis therefore proceeds by the search for patterns of internalised phantasy, internalised patterns of reality distorted to save a painful situation, which are shaping the present personal relationships of the group. So, for example, the patient's inability to accept reasonable orders from 'strong men' business superiors may be a pattern fixed in the mind, following a reaction to infantile experience with members of the family.[2]

There is in psychiatry today an emphasis upon the transference situation which was first described by Freud, but the idea of transference is not limited to the artificial psychoanalytic scene: this artificial scene is understood to be a special instance of what is going on continually in every social action of human beings. From the moment of birth, if not before, the child is reacting to other people and the products of that reaction remain in all concerned to influence the result of their next meetings. The model is not that of an isolated individual endowed with certain primitive pools of power, labelled 'instincts', which must be harnessed or burst their banks. The model is less mechanistic and more organic, less encapsulated and more diffuse. The present crisis that brings the patient to the analyst,

---

[1] Martin Buber's term. Cf. *I and Thou*, trans. R. Gregor Smith, T. & T. Clarke, 1957.
[2] Cf. Balint, M., *The Doctor, His Patient and the Illness*, Pitman, 1957, p. 69.

is seen not merely as stretching backwards in one straight chain of action and reaction within the patient to infantile experiences, but as stretching out to embrace the experiences of the patient's relatives and social group, and, through them and their history, to all mankind and all generations. The change in the models of thought is such that when the biblical model inspires such statements as 'For as in Adam all die, even so in Christ shall all be made alive'[1] this is for many modern psychiatrists a meaningful one whether they accept it as true or not. This understanding of the 'here and now', or 'present situation', as being at one and the same time an immediate particular crisis and a world-embracing event, equivalent to the modern theological concept of biblical revelation as judgment (Gk. *krisis*) in a particular human event of all human events,[2] is well illustrated by S. H. Foulkes, a leading authority on group psychotherapy:[3]

> The 'situation' is thus a total event, the parts of which add up to something less than the totality; it is constantly in a state of flux; it is a system of relationships displaying a flexible pattern of configurations; and it is organised about some focal point or points which are in reciprocal relationship to each other. Some workers, having limited the concept, in time, to the present have also limited it, in space, to the external observable environment, leaving the inner historical world of the individual out of the picture. For the group psychotherapist the situation stretches infinitely in all directions. The situation is a miniature representation of the world at large which is coterminous and continuous; the patient is seen extending in time to earlier selves, and inwardly to less conscious areas of his personality. The individual is therefore observed against a more extensive background than is usual in other institutions where behaviour is studied.

And again:

We can go still further and say that in our observations none of the disturbances we have mentioned are really confined to the person who comes to us as a patient. They are not simply a function of his individual personality, not even in their symp-

[1] 1 Cor. 15:22.
[2] Cf. Hazelton, R., *Providence*, S.C.M. Press, 1958, p. 128.
[3] *Group Psychotherapy*, Penguin, 1957, p. 30.

tomatic aspect, but are a function of a whole nexus of relationships between people. For example, a marital disturbance is always a matter between at least two people, and, as soon as we study the conflicts between this couple, we find that it involves each partner's earlier relationships to his or her parents and brothers and sisters. Again we may find that the irritating mother-in-law only reacts to the original couple in the way that she does because her own father, brother, or son is involved, and so the expanding network of implicated relationships grows. Even to describe adequately the simplest case, we could almost say even to describe a single symptom, we have to refer to an interacting network of human relationships from which it grows.[1]

There is, then, in the fields of mental hygiene and mental health services a new emphasis on the inter-relatedness of men and women, an emphasis which is leading to vast changes in the organisation of these services; changes of which the following will serve as examples.

1. *The organisation of an artificial full-time therapeutic community*

This is well exemplified by the work of Maxwell Jones[2] in the Industrial Rehabilitation Unit at Belmont Hospital in Surrey to which patients are admitted to join the community for some months. Two types particularly mentioned are those with neurotic heart symptoms which disable them, and chronic unemployables. The patients are made to feel that their problem is the concern of the group and that the concerns of the community are their concerns. A permissive, democratic, atmosphere is encouraged, and the treatment of the patient is not portrayed as being the responsibility of a few specialists, but as rather that of the nurses, domestic staff, and other patients. The organisation and discipline of the community is made the work therapy of the patients, and the reactions of members of the community to each other, and the organisational and disciplinary situations, are made the discussion material for self-analysis of the groups in the community. Every aspect of the community life is considered as relevant to the therapeutic aim, whether it be canteen

[1] Ibid., p. 78.
[2] Jones, Maxwell, ed. *Social Psychology: a Study of Therapeutic Communities*, Tavistock, 1952.

organisation, a breach of discipline, personal antipathies, or personal problems. Encouraged by the special conditions of community acceptance and community support the patient learns to see his 'illness' as a situation between him and society, and having resolved it in this special community, to return to his outside world community without resuming his former unsatisfactory responses.

2. *The reappraisal and reorganisation of existing mental hospitals*[1]

This is well illustrated by Caudill's study of the Yale Psychiatric Institute.[2] The traditional framework of a mental hospital remains, and the main task of the hospital is still seen as bringing physical and analytical aids to the individual patient, together with the maintenance of necessary distraints; but there is more awareness that the efficacy of these measures can be largely increased or diminished according to the community background of the hospital. So that what is going on between patient and patient, doctor and doctor, doctor and administrator, nurse and nurse, patient and nurse, nurse and doctor, is all important. In particular, there is an awareness of the dangers of the mental hospital becoming a community in which the norms of social behaviour are such as to encourage rather than remedy what are defects from the point of view of the norms of the outside society.[3] Everywhere, then, patients are being encouraged to continue, or resume, in hospital, acts of responsible decision in work and play, to the best of their ability, through constructive work in hospital and outside, through democratic organisation of their own recreation, and through participation whenever possible in the acts and decisions which keep the hospital running. The patient is given a status and a role in the hospital community which expects something responsible and creative of him, and which encourages his personal and social abilities, and not merely a sick status and role, which encourages and fixes his deficiencies; a

[1] Cf. W.H.O. Technical Report Series, No. 73. *The Community Mental Hospital*, W.H.O., Geneva, 1955 and Martin, D. V., *Experiment in Psychiatry*, Bruno Cassirer, Oxford, 1962.

[2] Caudill, W., *The Psychiatric Hospital as a Small Community*, Harvard, 1958.

[3] Cf. E. M. Gruenberg's essay 'Socially shared Psychopathology' in *Explorations in Social Psychiatry*, ed. Leighton, Basic Books, New York, 1957, and also *Institutional Neurosis*, Barton, R., Bristol, 1959.

sick status and role to which he may conform, thus coming to share the psychopathology of the patients who were present in the ward to which he was introduced.

3. *The treatment of patients in or at mental hospitals whilst leaving them partially or completely in their normal society*

This step follows logically from the last. The admission of patients to a mental hospital is regarded as a last measure, to be taken only when it is quite impossible to provide out-patient treatment. This is well exemplified by the Worthing experiment[1] in which it was found possible to reduce hospital admissions considerably by concentrating on out-patient treatment, backed up by domiciliary consultation service in the patient's home. The authors stress that the co-operation of the relatives is essential, for 'Our patients are not in hospital under trained observation, but they are at home with their families. Unless the relatives are prepared to work with us, and to accept some responsibility for the patient the case is unsuitable for out-patient treatment.' Another variation upon the same theme is the day hospital, which the patient attends daily, returning home each night, and the night hospital where the patient sleeps in the hospital or hostel, but goes out each day to work. There is, too, the week-end hospital where the patient spends five days in normal living and is admitted each week-end for treatment, sometimes even with his whole family, if the patient's problem is considered to be a family symptom.

4. *The treatment of the patient through the social group to which he normally belongs*

This is the next step in the process outlined. It is most common in child psychiatry, in behaviour problems of early years, where the natural interest of the parents makes it possible to gain their co-operation in self-examination and self-change for the benefit of the child. Parents, individually and in groups are helped to see their children's symptoms as family symptoms, the removal of which is a corporate concern, often involving some changes and suffering in others than the patient. The patient's neurotic symptom, his complaint, is part of the family

[1] Carse, J., Panton, R., and Worth, A., *Lancet*, 1958, 1.39.

equilibrium, part of its homeostasis, and therefore is serving a purpose for the whole family, bringing the family some 'secondary gain'; and therefore the resistance to the removal of his symptoms may come not only from the patient, but from the whole family. Thus the excessively dominant mother and the excessively dependent child are one; if the child is encouraged to independence without giving the mother insight into the situation, it may merely accentuate the mother's anxiety, and by increasing the hidden conflict between mother and child make matters worse. In later life, choice of a marriage partner may sometimes be largely determined by the needs of a neurotic defect in both partners, and removal of that defect in one partner alone may break the marriage. All social relationships are based on some kind of equilibrium, and change on one side of the equation demands change upon the other if the new equilibrium is to be stable.[1]

The Amsterdam Domiciliary Psychiatric Service is a similar demonstration of the trend to treat patients in their own home whenever possible, though in this case it is accomplished more by personal visits of the specialist and his staff to the sick man, and thus by giving support to him at the point where his problems arise.

Lastly may be mentioned the world-famous village of Gheel in Belgium, which since the thirteenth century has boarded insane men and women in its farmhouses and peasants' cottages, the patients being under medical surveillance. The patron saint of the village is Dymphna, the patron saint of the insane, and it was as a religious work that the care of the insane had its inspiration. The village is remarkable for its demonstration of the possibility of founding a community which can carry with it, without undue anxiety, and with very rare mishaps, severely psychotic patients.

From considering the treatment of the mentally sick through the medium of the group to which he belongs, it is natural to proceed to the prevention of mental sickness through the provision of a mentally healthy social environment. At the moment the main emphasis in this field is placed upon the early

---

[1] It is interesting to consider St Paul's words 1 Cor. 7:12–16, where he talks of the effect of the unbelieving husband on the wife, and the unbelieving wife on the husband.

formative years, and its influence is most felt in the fields of mothercraft, and the personal and social action recommended to deal with the deprived child. Here again the emphasis is shifting from the institutional treatment of the deprived child, to the support and maintenance of the child's home, or the near substitution for it by loving foster parents. The provision of a secure relationship of love is seen not as an ancillary and optional extra for the health of the child, but as a vital necessity for the child and the future of society. So Bowlby in the conclusion to his *Child Care and the Growth of Love* writes:

> Deprived children, whether in their homes or out of them, are the source of social infections as real and as serious as the carriers of diphtheria and typhoid. And, just as preventive measures have reduced these diseases to negligible proportions, so can determined action greatly reduce the number of deprived children in our midst, and the growth of adults liable to produce more of them.[1]

It is in the field of psychiatry that appreciation of the social pathology of disease is most prominent. The patient in hospital is seen as a 'situation' which involves not only his personal psychiatric history, his personal, medical, and socio-economic history, but also one involving a much wider society, and that society's history. Just as the child with a behaviour problem is seen not only as a person needing to make certain changes in his character, but also calling for changes in his parent, so the mentally ill adult is seen within the concept of a social neurosis, a sick culture. The consequence is that the psychiatrist, the sociologist, and the anthropologist find themselves continually meeting in their work. Moreover, because religious belief and practice is one of the determinants of the structure and behaviour of society, and thus a factor in the distribution and character of mental illness, it is of importance to the study of psychopathology. Finally, through the mechanisms of psychosomatic illness of which nowadays we are so very much aware, there is a linkage between culture and physical illness. We find once again in the field of psychosis and psychoneurosis, as in the field of geriatrics, that the quality of the local community is

---

[1] Penguin, 1953, p. 181.

of vital importance, not only in the carrying and nursing of illness within the community but also in the determination of its quantity and quality.

To appreciate the full significance of this fact, for the morbidity and mortality rates of the general population, it is necessary to grasp the degree of interaction between body and mind, and the frequency of psychosomatic symptoms in the general population. By 'psychosomatic' symptoms we mean symptoms in which a disorder of the psyche is a predominant factor in the aetiology of the symptoms. Possibly this term psychosomatic may be deemed unfortunate, tending as it may 'to perpetuate exactly the thing that one would wish to have eliminated—the idea that mind and body are fundamentally different. The very juxtaposition of the two syllables "psych" and "soma" brings to the mind of many people the connotation of "mind v. body". "Psychosomatic" medicine, therefore, might better be called "holistic" or comprehensive medicine.'[1]

Whatever the correct term, all authorities are agreed that the number of clinical conditions in the treatment of which attention to emotional problems deserves high priority, is increasing. Thus whilst there are very wide differences of approach between organicists and psychotherapists, both schools of thought, in practice, increasingly concern themselves with the social relationships and emotional lives of their patients.

Whilst the difficulties of delineating psychotic, psychoneurotic, and psychosomatic symptoms from organic diseases have led to wide diversities in the estimation of psychosomatic and psychoneurotic diseases amongst the general population, all authorities find that the incidence is considerable. Thus some recent estimates are: Watts and Watts[2] 20 per cent, Finlay[3] 20 per cent, Mestitz[4] 26 per cent, Kessel[5] 9 per cent. All general practitioners agree in finding that psychoneurotic and psychosomatic problems are as important in their work as other major classifications of disease, such as respiratory or cardiovascular lesions. Moreover, because every illness is part of the experience

Loeb, Cecil I, *Textbook of Medicine*, Saunders, Philadelphia, 1955, p. 1645.
[2]Watts, C. A., and Watts, B. M. (1951) quoted by Finlay, *et al.*
[3]Finlay, *et. al. Practitioner*, 1954, 172.183.
[4] Mestitz, P., *B.M.J.*, 1957, 2, 1108.
[5] Kessel, W. I. N., *Brit. Jour. Prev. Soc. Med.*, 1960, 20.

of the patient, and of those who come into contact with him, it follows that there is a psychological aspect of the most organic of diseases. Thus the speed and degree of recovery even from broken bones is affected by the morale of hospital, ward, and patient, to a degree which is not accounted for solely by the concomitant availability and utilisation of physical methods of treatment.

When we give due emphasis to the unity of body and mind which 'holistic medicine' demands, we begin to appreciate how the quality of the emotional life of the individual, and the quality of the community life in which the individuals participate, is vital not only to the quality and quantity of physical care which they may enjoy, but also to the quality and quantity of illness to which they may be subject. A man's peptic ulcer demonstrates not only the deficiencies of structure in the wall of his duodenum, not only deficiencies of activity of his digestive tract, not only disorders of his whole body, influenced by the relation between his cerebral cortex, his vegetative nervous system, and his hypothalamus, but his relationship with his wife. He may be bearing about in the body the ulcer of his wife's social ambition to out-do the Joneses, which in turn reflects childhood experiences of poverty and grave social injustice. Pressures of society through groups, in office and at work-bench, school and church, bringing possibilities of futile or creative relationships for the individual, may mar or make a man's health. Individuals by their experiences and decisions contribute to the experiences and decisions of the group in which they participate, and their state of sickness or salvation may be claimed to be in part positively related to the spiritual state of the community. Some recent investigators into the mental health of the residents in a new housing estate to the north of London reported a high incidence of mental illness and suggested that, 'each family keeping to itself generates a degree of loneliness and social isolation inconsistent with mental health.'[1]

There are many observations in medical practice generally, and psychiatry in particular, that support the belief that there is

[1] Brotherton, J. H. F., Marten, F. M., and Chance, J. H. F., *Brit. Jour. Prev. Soc. Med.*, 1957, 11.196.

some kind of relation between disease and culture. But whereas many religious people will rush in where angels fear to tread, and assert that it is a particular religious belief and practice that is the relevant factor, it must be emphasised that there is, as yet, scanty data on this subject, and that what there is gives little support for this claim. The absence of research in this field is most striking, but not perhaps very surprising, considering the difficulty of measuring those qualities which are alleged to be of importance. What are the degrees or units of measurement of love, intolerance, acceptance, anxiety, and inter-relatedness? It is possible, of course, to gather statistics showing the incidence of particular symptoms amongst certain broad categories of people, such as, say, Jews and Catholics, Americans and Chinese, though difficult to ensure that these groups are in other ways comparable. From such studies there is some support for the assertion that culture influences the outward and visible signs of inward and invisible failure to cope with stress. So that the Irish take to drink, Jews to psychoneurosis, Protestants to compulsive good works, and Malays 'run amok'! Eleanor Laycock in the summary of her essay 'Three Social Variables and Mental Disorder'[1] says:

> Incidence data on mental illness in relation to cultural background, although thin, do indicate that culturally patterned outlets for stress can affect the relative distribution of different illness categories in a population. However, at this stage this can only be said to apply at a relatively superficial level. Cross-cultural comparative studies have not reached the place where statements can be made about cultural background and personality malfunctioning on deeper levels.

However, clinical experience in general practice suggests that adult mental ill health is related to reaction patterns delineated in early years of life, and that the predominant forces shaping these reactions are personal relationships in which love, tenderness, acceptance, and other such qualities are vital. These clinical experiences need the support of data from large populations. Such data will only slowly and painfully be acquired, so that in the meantime we must live partly at least 'by faith and not by sight'.

[1] *Explorations in Social Psychiatry*, p. 336.

CHAPTER 3

THE COMMUNITY IN THE OLD TESTAMENT

IF ANYONE READING the previous chapters has gained
the impression that the idea of man as essentially a social
being is the discovery of twentieth-century medicine and social
science, let him turn to the Old Testament. His opinion will
soon be modified. For the Old Testament is the book of a People
and Israel are the People of the Book. The very word 'Testament' is a translation of the word 'Covenant' which is used to
describe the relationship between God and his people. This
covenant is made by God at one and the same time with a
person and a people. Thus God says to Abraham 'And I will
establish my covenant between me and thee, and thy seed after
thee, throughout their generations for an everlasting covenant,
to be a God unto thee, and to thy seed after thee' (Gen. 17:7
R.V.). So this great act of God, upon which are based all the
later acts of God in the history of Israel, is an act made at one
and the same time to an individual and a people.

Throughout the Old Testament it is the story of God's dealings with his people which is told. God first creates a people, and
then leads them, sustains them, loves them, punishes them and
saves them; and through them he makes himself known to his
creation. The Old Testament is not to be thought of as just a
book of enlightening stories about interesting individuals who
have made a personal response to God, which response has led
to a reshaping of their lives, though this forms a part of its
contents. The great characters of the Old Testament are great
because they contribute to the greatness of God's Israel.
Through them Israel is physically propagated, defended from its
enemies, saved from the wrath of Yahweh, told of his com-
mandments, chastised, comforted, guided. So Abraham,
through faith, becomes by God's blessing, the father of a people;
and we are told how through his actions the future of Israel is

assured. These actions of Abraham include questionable deeds such as pretending to Pharaoh (Gen. 12:11f) and to Abimelech (Gen. 20) that Sarah is not his wife, and of complying with Sarah's demands that Hagar and her child should be cast out into the wilderness (Gen. 21:9ff). These things do not trouble the narrator, for what matters to him, is that Abraham is obedient to God in his purpose of founding a people, and thus rightly enters into his reward. This reward is well summarised in the words concluding the story of the sacrifice of Isaac. 'In blessing I will bless thee, and in multiplying I will multiply thy seed as the stars of the heaven, and as the sand which is upon the sea shore; and thy seed shall possess the gate of his enemies; and in thy seed shall all the nations of the earth be blessed; because thou hast obeyed my voice' (Gen. 22:17, 18).

The Old Testament narrators tell us that what God has begun with Abraham he continues with the later Patriarchs, ensuring the continuance and prosperity of his people through Isaac, Jacob, and Joseph. This involves such actions as the gift of a child to the barren Rebekah (Gen. 25:21), the deceits of the wily Jacob, and the deliverance of Joseph out of prison in Egypt and his rise to prosperity so that he can in turn succour Israel and settle them in the land of Goshen. God's continued blessing is shown in the continuation and increase of his chosen community, and it is this promised gift that each Patriarch on his death-bed passes on to his sons, as for example Jacob to Ephraim and Manasseh (Gen. 48).

Moses is called to be the great leader and law-giver of Israel, and his greatness is the greatness of the part he plays in God's mighty act of bringing Israel out of the bondage of Egypt, through the death of the Red Sea, and by the Covenant and Law of Sinai to the Promised Land. God calls Moses not for the sake of his own soul but for the sake of God's work with Israel. So the theophany to Moses of the burning bush (Ex. 3) is not primarily for his personal salvation at all, but for the deliverance of Israel out of the hand of the Egyptians. 'Let my people go' (Ex. 8:1) is the keynote of the whole range of messages and miracles of God performed by God through Moses in front of Pharaoh. The passover is the saving, not of individuals one by one, but of families (Ex. 12:21) and households

(Ex. 12:22) of God's people. So the Passover, which later became for the Jews the type of all salvation, is a corporate communal event. The Passover meal of Judaism is the celebration and recital of the same historical event; it recites that this is how God does save and has saved men and women; not one by one, but by families and households. 'And it shall come to pass, when your children shall say unto you, What mean ye by this service? That ye shall say, It is the sacrifice of the Lord's passover, who passed over the *houses* of the children of *Israel* in Egypt, when he smote the Egyptians, and delivered our *houses*' (Ex. 12:27). The Passover and the Exodus which followed, the Covenant and the Law of Sinai, and the eventual gaining of entry into the Promised Land are all the story of God's dealings with his chosen community. These events are not peripheral but central to the whole Bible community experiences.

There is throughout the Old Testament a steady insistence that families, villages, cities, and nations are under a kind of group contract with God. The action of the individual, more especially if he be acting as a group leader or representative, whether as patriarch, father, king, priest, or prophet, carries with it possibilities of blessing or punishment for the whole group. The action of the group as a group in matters of justice, morals, and worship brings blessings or punishment for all the group including the individual abstainer. 'This collective responsibility implies that a man may be held responsible both as an individual and as a member of the community, even if he is not directly guilty personally.'[1] Whilst the importance of the individual, personal relationship of the one soul with God is never wholly excluded, and indeed receives considerable mention in Jeremiah, Ezekiel, the Psalms, and the Wisdom literature, it is fair to say that this individualism is never the only theme. The perfection of a symphony embracing these themes, joined together with another theme, only just touched upon in the Old Testament—the Suffering Servant—awaited the Master of the New Testament.

The Old Testament, in its general theme of a chosen people, in its record of the history of that people, of God's dealings with them, and their responses to him as a people, long

[1] Vriezen, T. C., *An Outline of Old Testament Theology*, Blackwell, 1958, p. 324.

anticipated the modern discovery of the large extent of man's physical and psychical interdependence. It is not, however, only in the plot and characterisation that the Old Testament demonstrates the corporate modes of thought of the Hebrew mind. The whole mode of thought of the Hebrew mind tends to be holistic. In contrast to the Greek mind it does not make those sharp distinctions between the individual and the species, the one and the many, a whole and the constituent parts, which is natural in our modern minds. The philosophical problems of the relative values of individualistic and communistic ways of thought, with which we are familiar, did not trouble the Old Testament writers, because they were secure within their own holistic way of thought. So basic to the Hebrew thought form is 'total thinking', 'holism', 'corporate model concepts' or whatever we choose to call it, that it permeates the whole grammar and literary style of the Hebrew Old Testment.[1]

The Hebrew concept of a totality, which is neither just a summation of discrete particles nor a mass arbitrarily divisible into parts, but a living organism in which the parts co-inhere, both giving and receiving strength and purpose is nowhere better demonstrated than in the use of the word *mishpāhā* (family) as a collective term not only for the human but all species. Thus Pedersen writes, 'All that forms a whole, a homogeneous community with its own characteristics, is a *mishpāhā*. Therefore, not only men and women but also animals left the Ark arranged in families (Gen. 8:19). Not only Israel but the whole world consists of families.' And again 'the idea of the *mishpāhā* is the basis of all definitions, and it immediately presents itself whenever the Israelite wants to define a community.'[2] So too Vriezen writes:[3] 'There is no essential difference in the Old Testament between the family and the nation: the nations are, as it were, large families and are often called by the name of their ancestors.'

---

[1] See Pederson, J. *Israel*, Books I and II, O.U.P., 1926, esp. pp. 106–13.

[2] It is appreciated that the overenthusiastic use of the work of Pedersen and others has led some theologians of recent years to lean too heavily on the distinction between Greek and Hebrew ways of thought and that this has earned just criticism, especially by J. Barr in *Semantics of Biblical Language*, Oxford, 1961. However, it is believed that sufficient truth remains about the holistic way of thought in the Bible to give ample support to our arguments in this chapter.

[3] Op. cit., p. 217.

The consequence of the important part played by the *mishpāhā* in the Hebrew 'model' of collectives is far-reaching, for the *mishpāhā* carries with it as a model far more than the 'organic' picture which typifies the model of most recent thought in reaction to the mechanistic straight-chain models of the nineteenth century. The association pictures of the biological models of today tend to be those of comparatively simple and primitive plant and animal life or partial physiological systems such as the hormonal systems of mammals. The unsatisfactory consequence of the application of such models to human sociological studies may be far-reaching. In contrast, the use of the *mishpāhā* model of collectives is to carry into all collectives, animate or inanimate, some qualities of the *mishpāhā* which suggest more than just the interdependence of one group of people at one moment of time, for the Hebrew family is extended in time and space to include all men. The whole Israelite people are like a tree rooted in their father Abraham, and the whole people of the world are a tree rooted in Adam. The tree is living now, so that even now the terminal branches are dependent upon the root, and Israel's strength centuries after the Patriarchs still derives from their meritorious deeds. When Israel sinned in the desert by their worship of the golden calf, only Moses' prayer to God to 'Remember Abraham, Isaac and Jacob thy servants' brought forgiveness for them. The descendants of a man depended upon him not merely for their procreation but also for continued life, so that if he were cut off from God they too would perish, like every branch of an uprooted tree.

The subtle implications of the use of *mishpāhā* as a model of collectives is illustrated by the close relation in Hebrew between *mishpāhā* (family) and *bēth ābh* (father's house) by which *mishpaha* gathers not only an extension into a fourth dimension of time, such as has just been mentioned, but also an extension into a fifth dimension of the spirit, both extensions being largely dependent upon the father.

For the Old Testament the family therefore extends outwards in space to all the families (nations) of the world, and it spreads backwards into the past to the Patriarchs. This is not all, for there is a vertical extension in the realm of the spirit. 'Israel knows it owes its existence as a people to God; he spoke to Abraham: "I will make of thee a great nation" . . . Precisely this spiritual origin of the people of Israel, which did not spring from a *contrat social*, or merely from a natural consanguinity, but from a spiritual relationship between worshippers of Yahweh, is the true explanation of its coming into being.'[1] The family owes its being, whether in small root group or large community, to the creative activity of God. He both begets them (Genesis) and names them (Covenant) to be his people, and their consent to be a family is not a *contrat social* alone, but an obedience to the Word of God.

The result of the close relation between Creation, 'family' and 'father's house' is that the Hebrew concept of a community, a group, or a collective is not merely of a present observable inter-reacting body, but of a body extending in time and space of which the present observable phenomena is an outward and visible part. There is thus not merely an 'oscillation'[2] between the individual Israelite and corporate Israel, but also between the Israel of today and the Israel of past history. Nor is this all, for the Hebrew model of a totality is not a mere extension in time and space of the smaller collective, but an indefinite extension in time and space through fatherhood of 'the blessing' received by obedient man from gracious God. Through this human obedience of man, God has chosen to channel his gracious creative power and it is this power—the blessing—which both creates the community and sustains it. The soil of God is not only the place of man's creation but feeds even the topmost and newest branches, which can only remain alive as long as they receive the 'blessing' of the power of life through the roots, trunk, and branches. This extension of the model of the organism, such as the 'body' or the 'vine' or a 'tree' into a fourth and fifth dimension of time and spirit is an essential part of the Hebrew concept of corporate personality. In determining the quality of this extension the Hebrew concept of the 'father' of the 'father's house', which is a 'family', is of vital importance. If fatherhood were merely another attribute like 'huntinghood'

[1] Vriezen, op. cit., p. 217.
[2] 'Oscillation' is described and defined in Shedd, R. P., *Man in Community*, Epworth, 1958, p. 38; cf. Knight, G. A. F., *A Christian Theology of the Old Testament*, S.C.M. Press, 1959, p. 176.

or 'eatinghood' the fourth dimension would introduce very little change; but for the Hebrew 'fatherhood' was a spiritual gift and a human participation in the Creation in which God made the Family and all the Families of the earth the very central part of the blessing of God upon man.

The 'father's house' introduces not only the fourth dimension of time but the fifth of spirit because the spread of community through him, the father, is a spread of the blessing, a spread not just of life according to the flesh, but a spread of the spirit—a life-line. The father is the lord (ba'al) of the family but not in the modern sense of one who 'lords it' (cf. 1 Pet. 5:3).

It is not necessary to discuss here whether or not it was the use by the Hebrew of such models as 'family' and 'father's house' for a collective which was responsible for the Hebrew view of a collective. Whatever its origins, the Hebrew view of a collective was such that when a man saw thirty sheep he did not see either 'a number of sheep' or 'sheepism', but both in a harmony created and maintained by the spirit of their ba'al. If this ba'al is withdrawn, it is like the withdrawal of gravitational force and momentum from a planetary system, resulting in either extreme isolation or coagulation. 'Although the individual in the Old Testament could be as truly an individual as any twentieth-century personality, the very conception of individuality was foreign to his thought. To be alone, to be separated from one's kind, and to live without contact with other men, that was the ultimate fear of Old Testament man. Even for a nation to live alone meant that in the end it became a 'non people' and perished off the earth (Deut. 32:21)'.[1]

One further subtlety of great importance is also introduced by the 'father's house', the concept of a head amongst equals, who as representative is dependent upon the family group, is rewarded and punished according to its obedience or disobedience, yet carries particularly within himself the power which the blessing has given him both to create a community and sustain it. The family is centred in the house, supporting the father through whom the family receives the blessing of God upon the family, and especially the blessing of abundance and

[1] Knight, G. A. F., op. cit., p. 27.

the extension of the family community. The father in the *mishpāhā*, the extended family which is the Old Testament type of a collective, is important because he introduces the concept of headship into the model of a collective. The importance of the particular kind of headship of the Old Testament father for the theology of the Ministry is obvious, and in so far as the Ministry of Healing is inseparable from the Ministry of Priesthood, all that is said about one applies to the other, but this is not our present concern. The 'blessing' of life, health, and abundance is given to the family, but it is given through the father. It is given to the extended family of Israel through the obedience of previous communities, but especially the fathers of Israel. The father is at once both representative of the house, and specially chosen and responsible. The Hebrew concept of the collective was such that it did not, and does not, lend itself to extreme forms of individualism, communism, or even of hierarchy, but embraces all these in subtle harmony.

We see therefore that the Hebrew mode of thought is strongly corporate and that the Hebrew model of community is that of a given unity rather than of numbers of singularities which the human mind makes into a unity. We are reminded of the modern discoveries of the Gestalt school of psychology and of the Jungian school of psychoanalysis. Of the former Stafford-Clark writes:[1]

> Originally perception was believed to be simply a process whereby the incoming sensory impressions, relayed through the nervous system, were assembled item by item like parts of a jigsaw puzzle and the final picture was recognised only when the assembly was complete. . . . There is now ample evidence to suggest that our brains are so constructed that we do not have to reconstruct complicated visual images from the constituent, separate, and unrelated impressions of all parts of our visual field, but rather that we tend to see certain patterns and shapes naturally, and in fact to pick these patterns and shapes out of whatever background may contain them.

By Jungians we are reminded of the theory of the collective unconscious in which all men share universal archetypes.

[1] *Psychiatry Today*, Penguin, 1958, p. 134.

In Jung's concept of the human mind, the individual mind shares in the life of generations upon generations of forbears. Deep beneath the level of the unconscious, preconscious, and subconscious mind of the individual is 'the racial unconscious', the shared but totally unconscious mental life of a self-contained community, their common hopes and fears, myths and dreams, of which each may be aware only at times and only in part. Still deeper stands the universal unconscious common to all humanity, upon which rests the whole mental life of mankind.[1]

The Hebrew concept of the community of man has much in common with these, but as Adam, the primal corporate figure of the Old Testament, shows, there is a peculiarly biblical attitude to the corporateness of man. The community of man with man is at once the work of God and the responsibility of man. Adam's own unity within himself, that is 'mankind's' unity within itself, remains only as long as Adam obeys the covenant of God. The consequence of disobedience is not merely physical hardship but family quarrel between Adam and Eve and consequent delinquency on the part of Cain. What God has done once he does again, and in Abraham he makes a new community, but here again the maintenance of the community depends upon the maintenance of the covenant. This is clearly stressed in the prominence afforded to the giving of the Law, and the solemn covenanting of Sinai. To the Hebrew all unity is created and maintained by the power of God, like a solar system in which the planets both came from the central sun and are maintained in their courses and in their relations to one another by its gravitation. When men break the covenant laws they break the grounds of their own unity and it perishes. Man's unity in the Bible is neither an accident of blind evolution, nor is it the non-individual part of man, a kind of universal soul, but it is the relationship between free men and women which is a concomitant of the same free relationship between God and his creature. Isolation from God and casting out from the community are not consequential one upon the other in the sense of the latter being the punishment for the other. They are concomitants. The social law may, of course, take 'casting out' action, but the individual who is 'cut

off' from Israel has already cut himself off. So it is that when
Christ, the New Adam, suffers and reverses all the work of the
Old Adam, his ultimate suffering and reversal is that of isolation
consequent upon Adam's sin. Christ identifies himself with the
isolate and experiences complete isolation from man and God,
and so before he cries 'It is finished' he cries 'My God, my God
why hast though forsaken me?' So too his victory is one which
re-establishes in him the coinherence of unfallen creation
(Col. 1:15–19).

Here it is vital that we recognise the fullness (*pleroma*) of
Christ. He is not only the redeemer of men in their personal
religious and moral aspects, nor only redeemer of the world
in the sense of redeemer of all men in their personal moral and
religious aspects, but redeemer of the whole created order. His
incarnation is not only into the mental and moral aspects of
man (Apollinarianism) but he is made flesh and therefore his
Incarnation is into fallen creation, and this is followed by his
Resurrection and Ascension in which he goes before us, the
first fruits of a new creation, until he is all in all when all
Creation is re-created.

CHAPTER 4

THE NEW TESTAMENT AND
THE COMMUNITY

MUCH OF THE WORK of New Testament scholars during the last fifty years has been directed to getting behind the scriptural text to the minds of those who witnessed the life, death, and resurrection of Jesus Christ, and of those who subsequently preached, talked, wrote, read, or heard about these events. These scholars, appreciating that the full meaning of the New Testament could only be understood against the background of the contemporary culture, have set themselves the task of first discovering what the drama may have meant to the actors and the audience of those days, before attempting to determine their meaning for us today. The consequence has been a realisation that a sympathetic understanding of Jewish culture of the first century A.D., and especially of the literature of that culture, is a necessity for New Testament study. Jesus himself, the majority of his disciples, his popular audience, his religious antagonists, and the majority of the New Testament authors were all Jews. Thus the Old Testament, the very centre of the life of Judaism, is, as its name implies, the preparation for the New Testament which fulfils it. The imagery of the Old Testament, its stories, its lessons, and above all its prophecies and promises, were part of the unconscious culture of the minds of those who took part in the great drama of Palestine. This is no accident, but is inevitable, because so much of the Old Testament is a record of God's dealings with his people and his promises to them, some already fulfilled, but most still awaiting 'The day of the Lord'.

A considerable proportion of the Old Testament concerns itself with this 'day of the Lord', the coming of the Kingdom of God, when the rule of God over his world would cease to be *de jure* and become *de facto*. The prophets warn the Jews of the imminence of the day when God's righteousness cannot but be manifested in his wrath against all unholiness. The apocalyptic writers describe in detail, couched in vivid symbolic language, the events before (the 'last days') and during, the last day ('the day'). The undiminished authority of the prognostications of the earlier prophets and apocalyptists leads to an increasing complexity, for all unfulfilled prophecy must be fulfilled, and the association images of the symbols multiply with each new usage. Amongst the speculations about 'the day', especially in the inter-testamentary period, were many about the part that might be played by the great national leader in bringing Israel to the satisfaction of their eschatological hopes. It was frequently asserted that God would choose a deliverer, as he had in the past chosen Moses, Joshua, David, and other great leaders to bring Israel out of captivity to the enjoyment of the fullness of the promised land. In particular, the unfulfilled promises of God to David, who was God's own chosen anointed one (Hebrew 'Messias', thus R.V. 'Messiah' and 'Christ' from the Greek Old Testament), as recorded in Scripture (2 Sam. 7: 16 'Thy throne shall be established for ever'), played a large part in this hope. A Messiah would deliver Israel from the feet of her conquerors, and usher in glorious last days, of which the remembered splendours of the Davidic Empire of the ninth century B.C. were but a miniature prototype. The consequence was, that when Jesus did works which were those popularly and ecclesiastically associated with the Messiah and the day of the Lord, he invited the question, 'Art thou the Messiah?' or 'Art thou he that cometh, or look we for another?' To this last enquiry, by John's servants, he replies: 'The blind receive their sight, and the lame walk, the lepers are cleansed, and the deaf hear, and the dead are raised up, and the poor have good tidings preached to them' (Matt. 11:3–5). Jesus here uses words which are meant by him to be reminiscent of the last day prophecies of Isaiah. 'Then the eyes of the blind shall be opened, and the ears of the deaf shall be unstopped. Then shall the lame man leap as an hart, and the tongue of the dumb shall sing: for in the wilderness shall waters break out, and streams in the desert' (Isaiah 35:5–6).

'The Spirit of the Lord God is upon me; because the Lord hath anointed me to preach good tidings unto the meek; he hath sent me to bind up the brokenhearted, to proclaim liberty to the captives, and the opening of the prison to them that are bound; to proclaim the acceptable year of the Lord, and the day of vengeance of our God; to comfort all that mourn' (Isaiah 61:1, 2).

That Jesus is using these words as a claim that the new age has come, and that he himself is the Messiah, is made doubly plain when he follows his reading in the synagogue at Nazareth of the passage from Isaiah 61, with the words, 'This day is this scripture fulfilled in your ears' (Lk. 4:21). Thus it was, that as Jesus went about preaching, teaching, and healing, every single thing that he did, and every word that he spoke, must have been measured in part, both for him and his witnesses, by their association with the Old Testament, and the messianic, and eschatological expectations of the 'day'. But this was not all; for once he had accepted his messianic role he began to interpret both it, and the character of the new age, in so radical a fashion that even his followers were astounded. Whilst unequivocally stating that he is greater than David (Mk. 12:35, quoting Ps. 110), he rejects the whole pomp of the Davidic model of the Messiah for one based upon the Suffering Servant of Yahweh (Isaiah 42:1–4; 49:1–6; 50:4–9; 52:13–53: 12). He rejects the imperialistic privileges of the Davidic model of the new age for one in which the elect are not recognisable by the way they 'lord it' over others, but by their royal priesthood of service (cf. Mk. 10:42–45).

Thus it is that those who witnessed the healing work of Jesus were not being called to observe only good deeds and moral excellence, shown in 'wondrous works', but were being confronted with the claim of Jesus that he was the Messiah, and that this was the Rule of God come amongst them. These are 'signs of the times', and as such, are not merely descriptive of what 'the times' are like, but are part of what is happening today, and of what will be the basis of the world tomorrow. They are 'effective signs' bringing in what they announce.

In the mission and message of Jesus Christ his healing work was not a secondary consequence, but the very means of the proclamation, institution, and enlargement of the new age, the rule of God. The healing work of Christ was not primarily a private work between man and God, an individual spiritual test and reward for a sick person, but an 'effective sign'. And, because those who witnessed it were present in it, and part of it, the healing work was a *public* effective sign'. Those who witnessed these works, were not just part of the audience, but part of the cast, not just a crowd but more like a Greek chorus. The healing works of Jesus are visible signs of the breaking through of the power of God, the kingdom, the day of the Lord, and therefore they are moments both of salvation and judgment for the community in which the healing work is done. The sickness-healing situation was a 'crisis' situation for the whole community group in which it occurred. The word 'crisis' is not used here in its modern sense of a severe temporary problem, but as a biblical technical term, 'judgment', part of the vocabulary of the Last Days. The Evangelists make it quite clear that when Christ healed someone, it was not merely a critical moment for the person healed, but a critical moment for the men and women who witnessed. They either had their eyes opened, and made a declaration of faith, or they closed their eyes and saw not, or they deliberately distorted what they saw, saying that it was not of God but another power (i.e. Beelzebub). The healings, therefore, were not merely effective signs in which Christ and the healed man were the sole actors, but effective signs in which all present took part, and not least those who scoffed. They were *public* effective signs.

1. *The healing works of Jesus as signs of Messiahship and of the coming of the new age.*

It seems wise, before setting out to demonstrate that the healing work of Christ was seen by him, his disciples, and the early Church as signs of his Messiahship, and the beginning of the new age, to make it quite clear that it is not intended thereby to claim that this exhausts their significance. In particular, there is no intention to belittle the saving effect, upon the lives of millions, of the imitation of Christ's loving work to the sick and rejected. The result of the fusion in the life of Jesus of the callings of 'Messiah', 'Son of Man', and 'Son of God' is not only to give his healing work a unique historic reference (*Sitz im Leben*) and a unique divine reference (Son of God) but also a general 'everyman' (Son of Man) reference. These three aspects of his healing work are recognisable but, like his person, are 'without change, without confusion, without separation'.

The difficulties for the modern man of reconciling the modern 'scientific' ethos with the description of signs and wonders which the New Testament attribute to Jesus are well known. The general result of this in recent years has been that, when the miracles of the New Testament have been discussed, this modern problem has quite naturally coloured consciously or unconsciously the whole approach of the authors or debaters. This—whilst natural enough, for the doubts of modern minds must be met where they are—has usually had the disastrous effect of leading to a complete neglect of the study of what Jesus himself, and those who witnessed and recorded the miracles, understood them to be. Modern discussion of the healing miracles has only too often unconsciously imported into the Palestine drama quite anachronistic viewpoints and problems. Thus, for example, it has been very often suggested that the onlookers and the early Church saw the miracles of Jesus as supra-scientific wonders, which, if accepted, were indubitable evidence of his divinity. This anachronism quite overlooks the fact that the working of such wonders was expected of certain people, even as today in certain parts of the world a good witch doctor is expected to be able to exorcise evil spirits which sicken and kill their clients.

From the biblical standpoint, and therefore in the assumptions of both Jesus and his witnesses, *all* power is supernatural. All power is from God, so that every observed phenomenon of nature, and every moment of history, exists only because he supports and sustains it. This power may be delegated to men and women, and especially to his chosen servants, or it may be abrogated by his enemies, but in the last resort he is the source of all power. If a man did exceptional things, as did Jesus and the 'children of the Pharisees' in their exorcisms, then they were exceptional 'condensers and conductors' of supernatural power, but they were exceptional only in degree and not in quality, for every human and natural act is sustained by the same power. Thus the Pharisees had either to recognise that the power which

they acknowledged to be present in Jesus had been given to him
as a servant, and face the implications, or to allege that it was
abrogated power that the devil, Beelzebub, had given to him.
Rather than face the implications they chose to claim, in the
very teeth of the spirit of their own sacred scriptures, that good
works were done not by God, but by the Prince of Evil (Matt.
12:24; Lk. 11:15). The question for Jesus' witnesses was not
whether a wonder had been performed, for this was a matter
which sensory experience could decide, but what the wonder
'signified'. What was it a sign of? Or to put it another way,
who was this man and why was he wielding this power? Jesus
does not conclude his dispute with the Pharisees, discussed
above, by claiming that he had done something magical, and
that this proved the existence of God. He does not say: 'If I do
an extraordinary, inexplicable, and magical exorcism, then
this proves that God exists and is here.' He says 'But if I by the
finger [Lk., Matt.: 'Spirit'] of God cast out demons, doubtless
the Kingdom of God is come upon you.' Thus Jesus tells them
what they already knew, the biblical logic of the situation, and
not modern 'miracle versus science' logic. He says to them 'If
you recognise.

(a) that Daemons have been exorcised and
(b) that this has been my work, and
(c) that I have done it by the Spirit of God, then it follows
    that
(d) the Day of the Lord has come'.[1]

He argues in word and deed with the Pharisees on their own
ground of biblical logic. The Pharisees do not here dispute (a)
or (b)[2] or that the consequences of (a), (b), and (c) are (d). So,
if they are to deny (d) they must deny (c); and this is what they
do, saying it is not by the Spirit of God but by the Devil that
this work is done. Therefore Jesus meets them on (c), asking 'If

---

[1] For argument for translating 'Kingdom of God', (ἡ βασιλεία τοῦ Θεοῦ) as 'The
Day of the Lord' and 'is come upon you' (ἔφθασεν ἐφ' ὑμᾶς) as 'has come' or 'is just
arriving at this very moment', see Dodd, C. H., *The Parables of the Kingdom*, Hodder
and Stoughton, 1936, whose 'realised eschatology' has been modified to 'imminent
eschatology' by later scholars.

[2] There is little evidence in the New Testament that they ever disputed the facts
of Jesus' healings. Jn. 9 records their sceptical enquiries, but suggests that they
reluctantly accepted the healings as fact, and this aggravated their problem,
especially after they heard the report of the raising of Lazarus.

Satan cast out Satan?' and follows it with some of the most terrible words in the New Testament (Matt. 12:31f).

The point of the controversy between the Pharisees and Jesus, as discussed above, was that Jesus by his miracles was fulfilling the 'days' foreshadowed by the prophetic and apocalyptic literature such as in the Isaianic signs. The lame walk, the lepers are cleansed, the deaf hear, the dead are raised, and the poor have the Gospel preached to them. These are the things 'that many prophets and righteous men have desired to see' (Matt. 13:17) says Jesus, shortly after answering John's disciples' question 'Art thou he that should come?' by pointing to his 'mighty acts' of healing. Thus Jesus, by his healing work, together with his interpretation of it by the repeated announcement that the Kingdom of God had come, was challenging all his witnesses to repent and believe unto salvation or, like Chorazin and Bethsaida, to turn away and disbelieve unto damnation.

The miracles of Jesus are powerful acts, mighty deeds, of such a nature that they are recognisable by the witnesses as signs of, and part of, the present rule of God. By these acted parables, Jesus at one and the same time *proclaims* the coming of the Kingdom, *portrays* what the Kingdom is like, and actually *initiates* and spreads the Kingdom. He does the same in his spoken parables of the Kingdom (i.e. Matt. 13:33f; Mk. 4:26f). Thus the gift of healing given by the Father to the Son was used by him to announce the Rule of God, to describe it, and to usher it in. Thereby he marked healing work done by all men in all ages not only, nor perhaps mainly, as imitation of his compassion, but as proclamation and description of the good news of the Gospel, the announcing and bringing in of forgiveness and salvation.

2. *The healing works of Jesus as effective signs*

The healing works of Jesus are not only 'signs' in the sense of indications, like signposts that point out a direction, or labels that identify an object. They are integral to the things that they demonstrate. They are not the diagnostic conclusions in the medical folder at the foot of the sick patient, but the signs and symptoms of the man himself. The regular pulse, normal

4

temperature, are 'signs' of health in this way, an integral part
of the healthy body itself. So Jesus' healing works are not only
pointers to his Messiahship and the Kingdom of God, but they
are part of it. Not only this, but they are part of a developing
situation, bringing about the very thing of which they are signs.
They are 'effective' signs. They not only are part of the rule of
God, but they usher it in and extend it. Jesus does not say 'If
I by the Spirit of God cast out demons, then this is what the
Kingdom of God will be like when it comes.' He says 'If I by
the Spirit of God cast out devils then the Kingdom of God is
upon you' (has come and is coming).

This concept of a sign which is also effective in bringing
about the condition which it signifies, is no anachronistic
sophistication of modern theology but a commonly accepted
occurrence in the Hebrew world. It is described by Old Testament scholars as 'prophetic symbolism'. Thus, when Jeremiah
makes a yoke and wears it around his neck, he is not only
symbolising the coming subjugation of Judah to Babylon, but
also 'taking his part in the actual working out of the Divine
purpose'.[1] Other prophetic symbols were Jeremiah's breaking
of the potter's earthen bottle (Jer. 19), Ezekiel's curious
actions with his beard (Ezek. 5), his house-moving (Ezek. 12),
and his city model making (Ezek. 4). This prophetic symbolism
is frequently met with in the New Testament, though often the
term 'acted parable' is used by New Testament scholars to
describe it. John the Baptist dressed himself in the traditional
likeness of Elijah (Mk. 1:6; cf. 2 Kings 1:8), and the Jewish-
Christian prophet Agabus bound his own hands and feet with
Paul's girdle, as a sign of the captivity of St Paul in Jerusalem
(Acts 21:10f). The ministry of Jesus is full of such 'prophetic
symbolism', 'effective signs', or 'acted parables'. He takes a
child and sets him in the midst (Mk. 9:36), he cleanses the
Temple, fulfilling the prophecy of Mal. 3:1–3 and beginning the
major prophetic symbol of his death and resurrection, in
which the Temple is destroyed and built again in three days.
He performs symbolic acts at the Last Supper, which both
demonstrate and institute the great supper of the last days;
but it is especially in his miracles that he is acting in the

[1] Dodd, C. H., in *A Companion to the Bible*, ed. T. W. Manson, p. 384.

tradition of the prophets. As Isaiah, obedient to the Lord's commands, walks naked as a sign of judgment to Israel (Is. 20:2f), and as Jeremiah and Ezekiel perform symbolic acts obedient to God's command to declare God's purpose to men, so Christ does likewise in his healing acts. They are obedient acts, done by the Son for the Father, which demonstrate God's will for the world and bring that will about. Like the prophetic symbolic acts of the Old Testament they are done in front of God's people, and they are intended to tell God's people of his immediate intentions, to carry those intentions into practice, and to demand a response from the people. They are *public* acts, *corporate* matters, *public* effective signs.

3. *The healing works of Jesus as public effective signs*

Christ's healing works have been the subject of intensive study and much debate of recent years. Usually, however, the motivation of this interest has either been centred in the science-religion controversy or else in the possibility of similar 'miraculous' healing today. The result of the first approach has generally been to transpose anachronistic modern cosmologies into the Hebrew cosmology of the times of Jesus, with the consequent disastrous misunderstanding of the healing miracles which we have already discussed. The result of the second approach has been to transpose the modern interest in the predicament of the desperately sick individual and the possibilities of his obtaining relief by appropriate personal acts of faith, on to Christ's healing miracles. This neglects the fact that, for the Gospel writers, the person who was healed, his personal religious attitudes and his personal response to healing, is secondary in importance to the attitudes of those who witnessed the healings. Great play has been made, and rightly, of the crisis for the individual sick man of being confronted by Christ, and of the need for his faith and repentance, and that the end result intended is his salvation and making whole, but in this excessively individualistic approach the corporate aspect has been overlooked. The healing works of Christ are prophetic symbols, in which Christ, the prophet, obeys the Lord's commands to 'Go and tell my people', only here it is not a wooden yoke, or a potter's vessel, or two sticks that form the 'props' of the scene. The 'props' here are 'representative sick man', and 'my people' are those present at the healing. The healing miracles are public entrances of the Kingdom of God. The Kingdom of God is upon all those there and it is a great and terrible moment for them. The crisis is similar to that when God spoke through his prophets either in their prophetic oral pronouncements or their prophetic symbolic acts.[1] The word of God spoken through his prophets was always a crisis for those who heard. It always pronounced the wrath of his holiness upon their wickedness, and yet held out promise of salvation if his people would hear and turn their hearts in repentance.

It is not just a coincidence, nor a pair of listed duties, that Jesus, when commissioning his disciples, commands them both to heal the sick and preach the Kingdom (Mk. 6:7–13; Matt. 10:1–15; Lk. 9:1–6; 10:1–20). To heal the sick and to preach the Kingdom are neither complementary, nor supplementary, but both are manifestations of the same word of God. When Jesus confronts men and women with powerful acts of healing he does not ask for mere wonder and awe; what he asks for is that men and women will recognise in the healing act a theophany, God's presence, his word, his finger. The response demanded of God's people when he appears is that they should repent and enter into the promises of the covenant. This is what God demanded of his people whenever he spoke through the prophets, whether by oral pronouncement or prophetic deeds and signs. This is culminated in God speaking through the prophet Jesus Christ in his words and his deeds, especially his powerful healings. Consequently when the spirit of the Lord is upon Jesus and this power is manifested to the witnesses of the word's healing acts, what is *required* of those witnesses is that they should fall on their knees, repent, and receive the promises. And what is *expected* is that some will do this, and thus accept salvation, and that others will scoff, and close their eyes, stop up their ears, turn away, and suffer the wrath of God's

---

[1] It is important to note that in the Old Testament God's verbal messages and his acts are not distinct. God's 'word' is his person acting towards his creatures and present to them in all his historical activities. So both prophetic words and prophetic acts are theophanies. God's word, 'power', 'spirit', 'finger' are all his presence. So Jesus is the 'word', 'power', 'spirit' and 'finger' of God.

holiness. This is what the evangelists are trying to show in their Gospel narratives; each successive move of Jesus, including his healing miracles, are successive moments of spiritual crisis for all men. These moves culminate in the final confrontation of the resurrection, but the healing works are of the same nature. St Peter sums it up (Acts 3:22 ff) when he says 'For Moses truly said unto the fathers, A prophet shall the Lord your God raise up unto you of your brethren, like unto me; him shall ye hear in all things whatsoever he shall say[1] unto you. And it shall come to pass that every soul, which will not hear that prophet, shall be destroyed from amongst the people.'

When Jesus does a powerful act of healing in public he is doing it in and to the public, in and to the community, and their presence and reaction are integral to the prophetic act. They are not spectators who just happen to be there.[2] Jesus is obeying the Lord's commands to his prophets, 'Go and tell my people'. Jesus *requires* his public healing acts to be received with repentance and acceptance of the Rule of God. Jesus *expects* that some will repent, but that others will shut their eyes, and stop up their ears, as Israel did to the prophets of old.[3]

The healing miracles of Jesus are therefore corporate effective signs. They are done 'in you', and they both heal and confront the community. They are signs of the Kingdom, ushering in the Kingdom, the rule of God, and demonstrating its nature. As the Kingdom comes upon the community, the power of the blessings of the mercy of God burst upon them and the wrath of the holiness of God judges them. When God visits his people, healing their sickness as manifested in the sick one amongst them, this divine healing is the time of their judgment, the moment of decision. The key to the full understanding of this is an appreciation of the Hebrew view of corporate personality which we have already elaborated. It is only half the truth to think of the miracles as being done 'in front of' the public. They are done amongst the public and within the community (ἐν ὑμιν) and they, the public, are in the sick man who is healed and he is in them. He is presenting and representing their illness, as a child's stealing presents and represents the enmity and

---

[1] 'and *do*' according to our argument above.
[2] Cf. Foulkes term, 'participant observers', op. cit., p. 29.
[3] Cf. especially Isaiah 6:8–10.

rows of its sinful parents,[1] or as Foulkes puts it, he is presenting in his disease 'the interacting network of human relationships from which it grows.'[2] Christ's healings are thus seen to be healings and judgment of the communities in which they occur.

[1] Cf. Bennett, I., *Delinquent and Neurotic Children*, Tavistock, 1960, p. 158.
[2] Op. cit., p. 78.

CHAPTER 5

THE REPRESENTATIVE 'CAST' OF THE NEW TESTAMENT HEALINGS

1. The healer as representative of the community.
2. The sick man as representative of the community.
3. The witnesses as representative of the community.

IT SEEMS WISE to commence by pointing out once again that in the light of the organic, communal models of thought of the Hebrew mind, a 'representative' means much more than a person who takes it upon himself, or is authorised, to put forward the views of a group of people. The modern usage of a representative in the political sphere inclines us to think of a representative as one who temporarily speaks for a group. We think mainly of speaking and voting, and we think of the person who is a representative as one who has for the time being adopted a role, as at other times he may be a butcher, baker, or candlestick maker. The representative is thus thought of as one who does something either 'for' those he represents, or 'instead of' those he represents. But in Hebrew and some modern organic models of thought the group speaks 'in' the representative. Similarly in recent psychotherapeutic thought the stealing child is not sick 'instead of' the mother or 'for' the mother, but the mother-child group is sick 'in' the child. In the Hebrew and modern organic models of thought, whenever the representative speaks or acts it really is the group he represents speaking and acting. It is not just a metaphor 'as if', but it literally 'is'. This view is, of course, modified in the Bible, and especially in the New Testament, by the affirmation of individual responsibility and of the personal relationship of each child with 'Our Father which art in heaven', but the corporate understanding still persists (N.B. *our* Father').

1. *The healer as representative of the community*

The representative aspect of Christ's work, in his passion,

crucifixion, and resurrection, is constantly dwelt upon in all authoritative discussions of the Atonement. Whilst there is considerable difference of opinion as to the exact meaning of 'representative' and the mode in which Christ's representative passion and death were an atonement, the majority of Christian theologians are united in the opinion that Christ himself, the Gospel authors, St Paul, the author of the Epistle to the Hebrews, the Petrine epistles, the Apocalypse, and indeed the whole New Testament accepted him as 'Man' in his atoning work. The theological literature on this is enormous, and no discussion of the Atonement, Baptism, Holy Communion, the Church or any other major Christian theme, ever should, and rarely does, fail to give this theme a real place. Whilst, however, the representative aspects of Christ's baptism, passion, and Atonement have received this emphasis, it is probably fair to say that there has been comparatively little attention paid to the representative nature of his work in the thirty years of his life between his birth and his passion. An exception is G. S. Hendry who recently wrote that 'The Christian Gospel, which is for our salvation, resides in the total fact of Christ and [that] it is inevitably distorted if it is made to hinge in an exclusive manner on one element, such as his birth or his death. In particular . . . the vicarious nature of the work of Christ is best understood if its ground is sought in the evangelical record of his incarnate life; in other words [that] neither his death for us, nor his birth for us, can be separated from his whole being for us.'[1] With a few notable exceptions such as this the representative nature of Christ's work tends to be limited by the use of non-corporate models of thought and therefore is usually seen as 'exemplary' alone. The '*imitatio Christi*' is, of course, an essential to the Christian life, and this thesis in no wise seeks to diminish its authority and appeal. But this does not exhaust the significance of any work of Christ, whether it be preaching, teaching, healing, living, or dying. As Dr Mascall points out,[2]

If the first stage in the re-creation of the human race is the assumption of human nature by God the Word, then *in some sense* what he assumed must be not an entirely abstract set of

[1] Hendry, G. S., *The Gospel of the Incarnation*, S.C.M. Press, 1959, p. 115.
[2] Mascall, E. L., *Christ, the Christian, and the Church*, Longmans, Green, 1946, p. 71.

human characteristics having no relation with our manhood except that of purely external and schematic similarity, but the actual concrete human nature which we possess. There must be more than accidental significance in the concreteness with which the *Te Deum* asserts that what the Son of God assumed in order to deliver it was not merely manhood but *man*. '*Tu ad liberandum suscepturus hominem.*'

Too often in Christian theology a Christian principle or dogma is based too narrowly on one particular action of Christ, or one particular part of his life. We shall have reason to speak more of this later when we argue that because Holy Communion is a remembrance (ἀνάμνησις) of Christ it cannot be thought of as only a remembrance of his death alone, but of his whole ministry, not least his healing work. Contrarily, too often a theological point, having been used to support one doctrine, is forgotten or dismissed on consideration of another doctrine. Thus it is with the 'representative' Christ. If, as the doctrine of Atonement asserts, 'man' or 'mankind' was crucified for us in Christ, must we not enquire whether 'man' or 'mankind' did not also in Christ heal the blind man at Bethsaida?

Jesus' own consciousness of himself as representative man

The most striking explicit reference by Christ to his coinherence with all men, is contained in his remarks about the Day of Judgment (Matt. 25:34ff).

The words here are not 'it is *as if* you had done it unto me' or 'it is *like* having done it to me' but 'ye did it unto me'. Nothing could be more explicit and emphatic.

Similarly emphatic, if not quite so explicit, are Jesus' words: 'He that receiveth you receiveth me, and he that receiveth me receiveth him that sent me. He that receiveth a prophet in the name of a prophet shall receive a prophet's reward; and he that receiveth a righteous man in the name of a righteous man shall receive a righteous man's reward. And whosoever shall give to drink unto one of these little ones a cup of cold water only in the name of a disciple, verily I say unto you, he shall in no wise lose his reward' (Matt. 10:40ff).

A parallel passage in Mark follows immediately after the

disciples have raised with Jesus the question of how they should view the work of men, not of their party, who are doing healing work (Mk. 9:38ff).

We meet the same thoughts of Jesus, identifying himself with all men, but especially with the wretched and the weak, in other passages. Typically the wretched and the weak are represented either by little children, or by the apostles suffering the hardships consequent upon their faithful ministry. Thus he says 'And whoso shall receive one such little child in my name receiveth me' (Matt. 18:5) and 'He that heareth you heareth me' (Lk. 10:16), and 'He that receiveth whomsoever I send receiveth me' (Jn. 13:20).

There seems to be no doubt that Jesus identified himself with all men. He felt himself to be representative man. But he especially identified himself with the following: those who sustained the downtrodden, the weak, and the sick; the downtrodden, the weak and the sick; those who sustained his disciples; his disciples who were servants of men.

There is here a most important 'foursome' of which it can be said that whilst some are always remembered when discussing the relation between Christ and healing, more often than not at least one is overlooked. In every encounter of man with man, in every giving and receiving, Christ's presence is fourfold.

He is the sick man, the prisoner, the child, the stranger.
He is the giver of the cup of water, the clothes, the visitor.
He is the one who preaches the Gospel.
He is the one who receives those who preach the Gospel.

Besides the explicit reference of Christ to himself as 'mankind' in those words already referred to, there is a similar claim implied by the titles which Jesus assumed and the role which he played. From the very first, by his messianic signs, he acknowledged himself to be a representative of his people the Jews. It is true that he had to break loose, and teach others to break loose, from the limitations of the popular conceptions of the Messiah as a politico-religious Jewish power figure; but his radical revision of the Old Testament and inter-testamentary insights into the nature of 'he who should come', was not done at the expense of the representative aspect of his

Messiahship, but by its development. Jesus does not reject the titles of 'Messias' (Mk. 8:29; Matt. 16:20) or 'Son of David' (Matt. 9:27; Mk. 10:47f; Lk. 18:38f). He reinterprets them, together with other titles of Son of God, Son of Man, and Servant of the Lord; and what he thus creates he teaches and shows forth in his life. 'Son of David' is not only a personal, individualistic title and role, but also a corporate title, for the king embodies his people, and they in turn embody him. Jesus is crucified 'king of the Jews', as all four Evangelists record, and thus, because the king of the Jews is the Jewish people, the Jewish people hang upon the cross in him and fulfil their mission as Servant of the Lord, to all peoples. Jesus by his acceptance of the title the 'king of the Jews' and 'Messias' and 'Son of David' accepted the Old Testament corporate aspects of these titles, and thus saw himself as identified with the Jews, and himself as the chosen of God, heir to their responsibilities, and their promises. When Christ heals, as when he preaches, and as when he suffers, he does so as 'the elect'. He is 'the chosen' to heal, to preach, and to suffer. He makes thereby acts of healing, preaching, and suffering, three effective signs, *corporate* effective signs, of election. In its healing, its preaching, and its suffering, a community enters into Christ, and with him into its election. The healing, preaching, and suffering of the community are at one and the same time both means of assuming its election and demonstrations that it has been elected.

It was this realisation in the mind of Jesus that his election was to something far greater and yet far humbler than either the Kingship or the Kingdom of David that shaped his life. He accepts the titles of Messiah and Son of David when others name him by them, but does not use them of himself. Instead, for reasons which the Gospels do not give explicitly, but which most scholars believe to be Jesus' refusal to have any truck with the popular desire to make him a nationalist politico-religious leader, he prefers the title 'Son of Man'. Certainly he is the Son of David, certainly he is the King of the Jews, but he represents them only in so far as they represent all men. Jesus prefers for himself the title 'Son of Man', and by his life and words tells us what that title meant to him, and what it should mean to us who are each, in him, 'Son of Man'.

This is not the place for a full discussion of the origins of the title 'Son of Man' as we find it in the New Testament, and we shall proceed from the following assumptions:

(a) that the title was truly the one Jesus used of himself and that it was not a later community invention;

(b) that its usage in the Similitudes of Enoch had little or no influence upon Jesus;

(c) that the usage by Ezekiel of the title—at least ninety times—had considerable influence on Jesus. There the meaning is largely that of prophet chosen by God to announce his judgment and above all his salvation to his people. The emphasis here is more on one chosen from amongst men to speak to men.

(d) that its use in Daniel was deeply meditated upon by Jesus.

Most commentators are agreed that in Daniel 7:13ff the 'Son of Man' represents the Jewish people, just as the beasts represent the pagan empires who suppress the Jews. The persecutor who arises after the ten horns (ten kings) is Antiochus Epiphanes against whom this secret tract is directed, and the 'saints of the Most High', whom he persecutes are the Jewish nation. We have here then a use of 'Son of Man' which has strong corporate suggestions, and above all is associated with the day of the Lord, when God will give dominion and power to Israel, the Son of Man, the 'people of the saints of the most high'.

We may therefore suppose that in Jesus' usage of the title 'Son of Man' we may look for this association of the rule of the saints of the most high, and that when Jesus says anything of the 'Son of Man' or does anything in this recognised vocation he has in his mind, amongst other things, the fact that it is of himself as the people of God, the saints of the new age, the chosen, the little flock, the Israel of God that he speaks, and it is as them that he acts.

The associations of 'Son of Man' in Daniel are then strongly communal and refer to a community which already has tasted the glories and powers of the new age, the dominion of the saints of the most high, the rule of God. The 'Son of Man' here, is one who represents the blessed, victorious, powerful, healed community of men and women of God.

(e) that the title 'Son of Man' is strongly influenced by the 'Servant of the Lord' songs of Isaiah (42:1–4; 49:1–6; 50:4–9; 52:13–53:12), especially the last. Also that whatever elaboration of this by the early Church may be present in the New Testament, it is a meditation on the original unique affirmation of Jesus himself that the Son of Man, prophet (cf. Ezekiel), Son of Man triumphant (cf. Daniel), and the Suffering Servant of the Lord, were all met in him and his mission.

We assume then that Jesus in his words and deeds accepted the vocation of 'Son of Man', and that his understanding of that status and role was deeply influenced by the certainty that they included that of the Suffering Servant. It is true that once Jesus accepts that status and role his every word and deed tells us what he (as distinct from modern commentators) thought about the Suffering Servant. Nevertheless we can still take note of recent discussions as to the identity of the Suffering Servant. In these discussions the Servant is sometimes said to be, amongst other things, an individual, such as Ezekiel, Jeremiah, Cyrus, Isaiah, Moses, the author of Deutero-Isaiah himself, or a future Messianic figure or a typical righteous Israelite. At other times he is said to be all Israel, or a righteous remnant, or an ideal Israel. The controversy between the individualistic and corporate schools of interpretation has been largely resolved by the realisation that rigid distinctions of this kind are foreign to poetry in general and the Hebrew grammar and culture in particular. We can assume then that in the mind of Jesus the 'Son of Man' incorporated a Suffering Servant who was an Old Testament symbol embracing a complexity of types both individual and corporate.

From the above assumptions it follows that when Jesus chose the title Son of Man, quite apart from the interpretation which he later lived into that title, he chose a title which had associations ranging from the specifically individual to the whole of mankind, from the one to the many. We may claim then, that when he healed the sick, he did it as the Son of Man, and as such the work was done at one and the same time by a specially chosen individual (cf. Ezekiel and the Messianic aspects of the Servant), by the representative of the chosen community (cf. the saints of the most high) and by humanity ('son of man'= Heb. *ben adam*, or *ben enosh*='Man').

It may be argued that whilst in the Son of Man concept there are both individualistic and corporate elements, it does not follow that these are always present in each 'Son of Man' saying, or at any rate always present in the same proportions. Vincent Taylor stresses the inseparability of the two aspects. 'In reality the Son of Man is never the community alone, and he is never only a person',[1] and 'Nothing could be more mistaken than to suppose that the application of the Parousia sayings to the community rules out the irrelevance to Jesus himself, or that their application to Jesus excludes their relevance for the community.'[2] But this does not preclude him from suggesting that the 'Son of Man' sayings of Jesus in his early Ministry are heavily influenced by the associations with the dominion of the saints of the most high, but that after the withdrawal to Tyre it is the suffering servant associations that predominate. This fact, that in his sayings and works Jesus may sometimes have largely thought of himself as primarily a chosen individual, sometimes just any man, sometimes all men and sometimes the chosen community, we do not dispute. It is the total exclusion of any one of these aspects that does so much harm, and we are here pleading that though Jesus sometimes, and perhaps even usually, in his healing work may have thought of himself primarily as *the* man chosen by God or *any* man chosen by God, he certainly also thought sometimes of himself in his healing work as *the* community chosen by God, or *any* community chosen by God.

We may conclude then that Jesus himself by his interpretation of his calling makes his healing work in some part at least a representative work. His interpretation of the Messiahship does not exclude the corporate element, and so for him the messianic healing work was a corporate effective sign. In him in Palestine long ago mankind took hold of its election and did a healing work which was a corporate effective sign.

---

[1] *The Life and Ministry of Jesus*, Macmillan, 1954, p. 176.
[2] Ibid., p. 177.

2. *The sick man as the representative of the community*

When Jesus was asked 'Who is my neighbour?' he answered with the story of the Good Samaritan (Lk. 10:30ff). In this story it is the Samaritan who is declared to be the *good* neighbour. He gains this commendation by recognising that a sick man is his neighbour, whatever his race, creed, or colour. The story shows that the stripped and wounded man is representative of the neighbour, regardless of whether or not he lives in the same close neighbourhood and belongs to the same class. Jesus himself, having spoken these words, must have regarded his own healing work as acted parables of the Good Samaritan type. They are acts done to all of his neighbours through their sick member.

We have already mentioned those passages in the Gospels where Jesus says that inasmuch as something is done unto a child, a sick person, a prisoner, or other deprived person it is done unto him. This too, because Jesus elsewhere, as we have just argued, sees himself as representative man, means that these same acts are done to representative man. They are done to the community.

A further instance of the representative aspect of the patient in Christ's healing work is in the selection of those whom Christ heals. The general impression we have is that Jesus, putting his preaching work first, had of necessity to restrict his healing work. Men and women were only too ready to come in multitudes to be healed or to witness healings. Thus Mark records that as a consequence of the unwanted publicity given him by the 'leper' he had healed, Jesus' work was impeded (Mk. 1:43ff). We can imagine how Jesus had to practise a vigorous selection of patients, and that in his humanity he had to carry the burden of disciplining his immediate compassion for the sake of his long-term objectives. The extent of that discipline is indicated by the fact that whilst no one will deny, and certainly not the Gospel authors, that Jesus had compassion on all sick men, and not least those whom he healed, the Gospels only occasionally suggest compassion as the criterion of selection.[1] Weatherhead remarks on the mixture of emotions that

---

[1] On the use of 'to have compassion', σπλαγχνίζομαι cf. A. Richardson, *The Miracle Stories of the Gospels*, S.C.M. Press, 1941, p. 33.

Jesus must have felt in the conflict between his compassion for the importuning leper (Mk. 1:40 ff) and his desire to follow his ministry as he conceived it.[1] He points out that some of the very human difficulties felt by Jesus are reflected in his outspoken language to the leper. Jesus, we may suppose, was certain on the one hand of the primacy of his preaching mission in word and deed, but on the other hand he knew that his onlookers would be only too glad to forget the need for repentance in the thrills of a healing mission. He must therefore have had rigorously to restrict his healing work. The selection by the authors of healing works for record in the Gospels probably therefore rests on an original drastic selection by Jesus. This in no way denies Jesus' perfect compassion for *all* sick men and women, but takes his humanity and its limitations seriously. The further selection of healing works for record by the evangelists and especially by the authors of St John's Gospel is not arbitrary but rests upon the mind of Christ. Because of his humanity Christ's healing work is selected in part by contingent factors of time and place. He submits to these, and it is Simon's mother-in-law who is healed of a fever (Mk. 1:30) and Mary and Martha's brother who is raised (Jn. 11), not just anyone, or necessarily even the most advantageous from the point of view of the Gospel preaching. Within these limitations of time and place, Jesus, having chosen to preach the Gospel in his healing work, must have made his selection of patients so that in them 'the work of God should be made manifest' (Jn. 9:1 ff, on the man born blind).[2] So we may say that the evangelists' descriptions of the healing work of Jesus as healing of representative men is rooted in the mind of Jesus.

We have already argued that the healing work of Jesus is to be understood partly at least as messianic signs. The eyes of the blind must be opened, the ears of the deaf unstopped, the lame walk, and the dumb speak. So those who are healed are representative of the sickness of men. Behind the Isaianic categories

---

[1] *Psychology, Religion and Healing*, Hodder and Stoughton, 1952, p. 52.

[2] This whole subject seems very relevant to the difficult problem of how the priest today can make a working rule by which to live his important role as a social adviser-psychotherapist in such a way as not to limit but fulfil his essential role as minister of the Gospel. Christ himself faced the same problem, only enormously magnified, because he had both greater compassion and greater power to heal. Christ's compassion for sinful mankind overrules the compassion aroused by the less radical needs of some of mankind.

of sickness lies a wealth of Old Testament association imagery, for the deaf, the blind, the dumb, the halt are representative of mankind in its fallen-sickness-sinfulness aspect. They represent mankind who cannot hear the word of the Lord, nor see his glory, nor speak good of his name, nor walk in his ways. Christ, when he opens a man's eyes is opening the eyes of the man's community for his blindness 'presents' their sickness. When Christ unstops a man's ears he is opening the ears of the man's community, for the man is 'presenting' their deafness. St Mark, immediately after reciting the giving of sight to the blind man of Bethsaida and the charge to secrecy, tells of the giving of 'sight' to Peter, and through him to his community of disciples, and the charge of secrecy to them (Mk. 8:22 ff). So too, the opening of the eyes of blind Bartimeus is the opening of the eyes of the blind community to see the public proclamation by Jesus of his Messiahship, just before his entry into Jerusalem (Mk. 10:46–52).

In St John's Gospel the process of selection of mighty works which is present in the Synoptists is carried further and made more explicit. The miracles here are most plainly signs and each one chosen to illustrate one special aspect of Christ's work. For St John, Jesus' healings were done 'that ye might believe that Jesus is the Christ the Son of God:[1] and that believing ye might have life through his name' (Jn. 20:31). St John shows most clearly what all the evangelists record, namely that the onlookers of Jesus' healings were expected to see the sick man as their representative, but the difference between the Synoptists and St John is one of degree not of kind. Thus the Marcan account shows the healing work of Jesus moving out from the first healing in the synagogue (1:21) representing worshipping Jews, through Peter's Jewish home (1:30) and the Jewish city (1:33), embracing the Jewish outcast (1:40). Later, a great step is recorded by St Mark in the account by Jesus of the Syrophoenician's daughter, who here represents, as all commentators stress, the Gentile world. Jesus, having first stretched forth his hand to cleanse worshipping Israel, and followed this by taking away the uncleanness of leprous, outcast Israel, finally takes the burden of the Gentiles. Thus Jesus and the

[1] Cf. Jn. 11:27 where Martha uses these words and her brother Lazarus has life.

Evangelists teach us to see in the sick man the community he represents. Christ himself and all mankind are present in every sick bed in home and hospital. Or to put it another way, Christ and mankind 'present' themselves in every sick man that 'the works of God should be made manifest in him' (Jn. 9:5).

To these arguments about the representative nature of the sick man in the Gospel stories must be added what is, whilst indirect, the strongest argument of all: that the Jews, and Jesus himself, regarded the relationship between sin and disease as extremely close, and that they had no doubts about the corporate nature of sin. The corporate concept of sin, which we find in its most extreme form in the Deuteronomic tradition, was modified by the special personal responsibilities of chosen historic figures. It was modified too by Jeremiah and Ezekiel, by Job and the Wisdom literature. However, even in its moderate form it was still emphatic and it persisted and was current in Jesus' day. The same can be said of the relationship between sin and disease, which the Old Testament always assumes to be very close. Though different questions might be asked about the sick man, such as 'Did this man sin or his parents?' (Jn. 9:2) or 'Were these casualties "sinners above all men"?', the general assumption of the close relation between sin and sickness still stood fast (Lk. 13:1–3). It is this, and neither a lack of humanity nor a denial that God did not wish to make all things good which made the Jews reluctant to interfere with disease, and to pay such little respect to physicians that their only mention (Ecclus. 38:1–15) is to damn them with faint praise. The Jews were only being consistent to their belief that the holiness of God, and the righteous wrath against sin manifested in sickness, could not be set aside without impiety. Thus Weatherhead correctly outlines the Old Testament attitude, and illustrates it with a quotation from the Rabbi Jonathan, 'Disease came from seven sins, slander, shedding blood, false oaths, unchastity, arrogance, robbery, and envy.' He correctly says, too, that whilst Christ 'did regard disease and illness as part of the Kingdom of evil' he did not believe that a sufferer's sickness 'was necessarily due to his own sins'.[1] But he goes too far when he speaks of Jesus as exploding 'the heresy which attributes

[1] Op. cit., p. 33.

illness to personal or family sin, a heresy which retarded the healing methods of the Jews before Christ's day'. This is to miss the whole point of the Gospel healings. What Jesus explodes is not the alleged heresy that illness is due to personal or family sin, though no doubt he would have modified this strong statement, but the Jewish 'heresy' that man's sin cannot be forgiven. The accepted logic which was prevalent was:

1. God is Holy and all evil is anathema to him.
2. Sin must therefore bring its just rewards.
3. Sickness in mankind is one such consequence.

Therefore:

4. To remove sickness without removing sin is impious.

But:

5. No man has authority to forgive sins.

Therefore:

6. Healing the sick is a dubious activity.

Now whilst Weatherhead is right in suggesting that Jesus may have made some modifications in (3), he is quite wrong and misses the significance of the Gospel healings when he suggests that it is (3) that Jesus attacked. Christ would never then have been crucified. He was crucified because he contradicted proposition (5) in his life and teaching, claiming that forgiveness was given to men upon repentance, and that he had the authority to proclaim that forgiveness. Nothing could be more clear than the Marcan account of the healing of the man sick of the palsy (Mk. 2:1–13).

(a) A man is sick.
(b) Jesus forgives his sins.
(c) The Jews say this is blasphemy, for only God can forgive sins.
(d) Jesus answers this by healing the sick man.

But this is an effective answer only if Jesus and the Jews agree that the man's sickness is closely related to his sin. Otherwise the only other explanation would be that Jesus was giving a sign which overrode for its sheer wonder the scepticism of the Jews, and that it was just a mere coincidence that he healed the man, when turning stone into bread would have served even better.

This interpretation is contrary to our knowledge of Christ's methods. Jesus' action shows his broad acceptance of the Old Testament belief in the close relation between sickness and sin. This relation was to a large degree a communal relation, in which all men share in each other's flesh and sin, and bear about in their bodies the consequence of another's sin—the sin of Adam (*adham*=man) results in the curse of man (Gen. 3). A social pathology of disease is a normative assumption in the Old Testament and the final aetiological factor is Adam's, man's, sin. Thus it is that we can say that the sick man whom Christ heals is representing the community in their fallen-sickness-sin situation. When Christ shows that the Son of Man is a sin-bearer, he shows that man is a sin-sickness bearer. Christ does not, as the modern mind would so often like to read into the Gospels, 'reject the heresy that sickness is the consequence of personal and family sin'. He accepts it and the consequences in Gethsemane, and makes what is a stumbling-block to the Jews and an offence to Greek minds (and modern Greek-influenced minds) the very corner-stone of individual and corporate redemption. It is by their response to the suffering of their representative who bears their sin, presenting their illness on cross or sick-bed, that the community is judged to salvation or rejection.

3. *The witnesses of healing as representatives of the community*

It is symptomatic of the usual modern approach to the healing miracles of the New Testament, with its preoccupation with the state of mind of the healer, and of the sick individual or his friends, that the main feature of the Gospel accounts is overlooked. This main feature is the response of the witnesses, including the patient, to the healing which has just been done. For the evangelists the healings had two main interests. First, what the healing proclaimed about Christ and what he was doing for men. Second, whether the witnesses understood what the healing proclaimed and how they responded.

So far has this main feature been overlooked that it has twisted the whole approach to Christ's healing works, and especially to the phrase 'seeing their faith'. Contrary to the whole New Testament usage of the word 'faith', this is often interpreted as a necessary psychological condition upon which the cure might be effected, but faith for the Evangelists was the God-given ability and willingness, to recognise Jesus Christ as 'my Lord and my God'. This faith was certainly a prerequisite for Christ's healing works, but not because without them Jesus could not free them from symptoms, but because there was no point in doing mighty acts if every one who witnessed them was blind, deaf, and dumb. It is true of course that 'faith' in the New Testament sense often includes psychological predisposition and intellectual assent to the proposition that Christ can heal—for Christ *is* the power of God unto salvation. And thus when Jesus says 'Thy faith hath made thee whole' we can be sure that there was present a feeling that Christ could heal. But this was no commendation except in so far as it was part of a recognition of the lordship of Jesus and acceptance of that lordship. Indeed it is precisely this fact—that acceptance of Christ as Lord leads to renewal of life in him—that was and is so often taught by the Church, using the healing miracles as texts. This tradition had already been at work thirty to sixty years when the Gospels were written and no doubt the stories of the healing miracles as we have them today were moulded in part by this usage. We can never be sure of the extent of this editing, but it is reasonable to suppose that it would be in the direction of laying stress upon the need for men and women to have faith if they were to be born anew in Christ. When the evangelists wrote the Gospels they would then understand the words 'Thy faith has made thee whole' as 'Thy faith in Jesus Christ as thy Lord and Saviour has made thee whole.' It would have been quite impossible theologically for the Evangelists to have used the word 'faith' as meaning anything else but 'saving faith', and a complete anachronism for them to have thought of it as 'a kind of psychological atmosphere'[1] favourable to a cure.

The classification of Christ's healings in terms of the presence in the patient or his friends or witnesses of a suitable 'kind of psychological atmosphere', whilst of interest, is likely to lead, and usually does lead, to a fatal neglect of the fact that these encounters between Christ the healer, the patient healed, and

[1] Weatherhead, op. cit., p. 72.

the witnesses, are eschatological. They are theophanies. The finger of God has stretched out and touched man. The Spirit of God has rent the veil of the Temple, and the witnesses can, if they do not close their eyes, see the Shekhinah. These are moments of judgment. To witness the healing work of Christ is a great and terrible thing because it places the witnesses 'on the spot'. The community, the crowd, the Apostles, the patient, were judged by Christ, who in every healing revealed the glory (δόξα). We shall argue later how this judgment continues in all healing work, however secular, but it is hidden and only made visible by the Holy Spirit when he reveals it by the action of the Church. A difficulty here for so many minds is that they find it difficult to associate judgment with love, and especially when the love is expressed in so benign an action as healing.[1] Splitting off judgment by the attribution in modern art of love to Christ, and wrath to the Father has both displayed and strengthened this misunderstanding. Similarly, in the study of the life of Christ the attribution of his prophetic, wrathful qualities to specific texts and incidents which can be conveniently pigeon-holed and forgotten, has enabled us to forget that Christ is most the judge, not with a whip in his hand, but in acts like his healing and his Crucifixion. St John nails this lie with his phrase 'the wrath of the Lamb'.

The evangelists, when they wrote their Gospels, were well aware of this eschatological aspect of the revelation of the glory of God in his Son's works, and how each successive unveiling of the glory intensifies the judgment. This conception of the unveiling, the revelation, as judgment (κρίσις) is part of the Old Testament where God's power (δύναμις) and glory (δόξα) is veiled except when Moses' face shone (Ex. 34:29–55; 2 Cor. 3:18). The unveiling, the full theophany, awaits the day of the Lord and the separation of the righteous from the wicked. The evangelists see this successive unveiling in the life and death of Christ, and with each new revelation of God's power and glory they know that the witnesses are being judged, and, through the witnesses, the whole of mankind.

---

[1] Nowhere is this more marked than in the 'permissive attitude' of psychiatrically influenced Christian healing circles. Christians should remind themselves that love includes judgment and use their theological insight to remind the psychiatrist that an adequate parental substitute must amongst other things be a judge.

Jesus says 'If I by the finger of God cast out devils then the Kingdom of God has come upon you.' We may understand this as 'If I by the power of God heal men and women, then now is the time you must choose between turning to God to receive all the blessings of a new life or turning from him to all the horrors of a dead life.' Because the healing acts of Christ are not just labels or lectures, but corporate effective signs, they do actually have the result, that as soon as they are done the community is judged. Then some are saved or made whole, whilst others are lost. Jesus points to this fact, that to witness his healing works is to enter into the beginnings of the day of judgment, when he tells the people of Chorazin and Bethsaida that their failure to repent upon seeing his healing work jeopardises their salvation (Matt. 11:20; Lk. 10:13). The evangelists in their accounts show the Pharisees and Sadducees in particular, and the Jews in general, being judged by their response to Christ's work. The Jews see God in Christ healing a man, and because Christ offends their idea of God, they say it is not God who has healed. The ten lepers see themselves and their comrades healed, but only one responds and is saved[1] (Lk. 17:12). The story suggests that it is the response of faith to the healing that he has witnessed and gained that leads to his salvation. The other nine have made no use of this opportunity of wholeness. They are in danger of being classed with Bethsaida and Capernaum who have seen these 'mighty works' and should 'have repented long ago'.

St John makes this fact, that to witness a work of God in Christ is to be 'put on the spot', quite explicit, especially in the story of the raising of Lazarus. The raising of Lazarus means that those who witness it are in the visible presence of God: but the visible presence of God in the Old Testament tradition is a consuming fire, so that Moses must not see the face of the Lord (Ex. 33:20) nor the Israelites the glory on Moses' face which must be veiled. St John shows that the consequences for those who witnessed the raising of Lazarus are as important as the consequences for Lazarus. This includes not only first-hand

---

[1] Actually R.V. 'made whole'. The story is valuable in showing that the faith which makes whole is something more than the therapeutically effective expectant attitude which all ten displayed. Freedom from symptoms does not necessarily mean that the nine lepers are any nearer being made whole.

witnesses, but all those, including ourselves, who experience it through the faithful witness of the Church. The result of the 'manifestation' or 'visible presence' of God in the healing of Lazarus is that 'many of the Jews believed on him' (Jn. 11:45) 'but some of them went their ways to the Pharisees'. The witnessing of Jesus' healing gives the men and women the opportunity and the power to crucify him. This they proceed to do (Jn. 11:53).

The healing works of Christ show that the communities of men and women who experienced them in themselves were confronted by the visible presence of God. Like all men and women who are thus confronted, they could not escape, at that very moment,[1] from judging themselves. Their response is their judgment, and their judgment is their entry into a better quality of life (new life, life eternal, etc.) or a worse quality of life (death, separation, darkness of the day). Either they suffer their eyes to be opened or they close their eyes to the light of God; as Jesus says after the healing of the man born blind, 'For judgment I am come into this world, that they which see not might see; and that they which see might be made blind' (Jn. 9:39).

The witnesses of healing works in the New Testament are as representative as the healer himself and the patient. They are the whole community of man, confronted by the visible presence of God in Christ healing men and women in their midst. Men and women have always been without excuse (Rom. 1:20) for not recognising the presence of God in such works of healing, but now they are given a new opportunity. Now is the time. Let them recognise in Christ's healing work the presence of God unto salvation; let them, like the man born blind, make the declaration of faith, 'Lord, I believe', or else their 'sin remaineth'.

We may conclude that for the New Testament sickness in an individual is a form of crisis which offers possibilities for good or evil to all who by necessity or choice are involved in that crisis.

---

[1] This 'here and now' runs through the healing miracles and all the New Testament. It is interesting to note the same in modern Existentialism and in much psychotherapy today, where it is the understanding of the psycho-dynamics of what is happening *now* between the participants, analyst and analysand, which is vital for progress.

Christ's presence, in perfect love, offers the widest possibilities to profit or lose in that crisis. To use the terms of an expert in mental health, 'crisis' in a group of people is a time of opportunity, for it will always end in a 'new equilibrium'. The quality of the 'psychological work' done by those involved decides the outcome. 'What we get at the end of crisis is new equilibrium. The new equilibrium, if the psychological work has been satisfactory, results in external adaptation and internal adjustment. If the psychological work has not been satisfactory, there is also a new equilibrium, but this equilibrium is one of regression. It is a regressed equilibrium in the direction of either a neurosis, a psychosis, or some form of alienation or disintegration.'[1]

[1] Caplan, G., *Community Mental Health*, Tavistock, 1961, p. 43.

CHAPTER 6

THE EARLY CHURCH'S CORPORATE EFFECTIVE SIGNS OF HEALING

W E HAVE ARGUED so far that Christ's healing works, considered in their representative aspect, showed that man's sin-sickness situation is communal as well as private. We have also shown, that God requires that men and women shall see the sick man as bearer of their own infirmities, and that they shall, as representatives of men in Christ, stoop to share this burden. As they do this, and as they bring comfort and healing to the sick, they must remember the Incarnate Lord's healing work, and say to themselves and to all men: 'Now is God present in us in love, and now is the time of salvation and judgment for us and for all. The Kingdom of God is come upon us.'

What Christ did in his healing work is thus to continue after his Ascension. His healing work looks both backward and forward—forward to the healing work of the Lord the Spirit[1] in his whole Body, backward to the work of the Lord of the Spirit stirring men's hearts to compassion throughout the ages. The Lord the Spirit, who 'at sundry times and in divers manners spake in time past unto the fathers by the prophets, Hath in these last days spoken unto us by his Son' (Heb. 1:1-2 A.V.), but what in times past was veiled, and today is veiled, is unveiled by the witness of the Spirit in the Church to the healing ministry of Christ. The Lord the Spirit is working in the hearts and minds of men and women, stirring them up to lives of healing and compassion in hospital duties and trained social work, and lay works within the community. This veiled activity of the Lord the Spirit within a secular and sometimes pagan culture,

---

[1] I use the title 'the Lord the Spirit' of him we commonly call 'The Holy Spirit' because it helps to correct the almost universal misconception that he is an 'it'. Together with the concept of 'the Whole Body' I hope by this to prevent a Christocentric thesis from becoming Christoterminal, and the idea of coinherence in Christ from becoming ecclesiastically confined. The title 'the Lord the Spirit' I take from Charles Williams's magnificent book *The Descent of the Dove*, Faber, 1950.

is unveiled by the work of Christ, declared to be what it is. This witness to Christ is the work of Christian faith today, for though God's activity in the Lord the Spirit does not wait upon the recognition of his activity, the recognition of that activity is the work of men and women by faith in Christ. Nor is this act of faith a mere formality which leaves the situation unchanged, but it makes available all the fruits of the activity of the Lord the Spirit. To use a very rough analogy from physical medicine: the making explicit to doctor and patient of what the one is doing to another in the matter of injections, operations, investigations, etc., is not merely a formality but is vital to the efficacy of the therapy and indeed it is part of the therapy. So to declare in faith in Christ that the Holy Spirit is at work in, say, a pagan physician's professional dedication to his patient is not to leave the situation unchanged. It changes the situation and makes possible further changes, as all concerned accept or reject the Gospel witness. We may use another analogy from medicine, this time from psychotherapy. The recognition by a patient of the motivation for physical symptoms and attitudes to the therapist is no formality, but at once means a new level of diagnosis and possibility of healing. Indeed the very moment of recognition is the moment of first healing, as the patient dares to let go his defences and dares to expose himself to the love and judgment of another.[1]

The healing work of God in Christ is then an unveiling to faith of God's unchanging love and compassion, of his impassable concern for his children, unveiled, but still only seen by faith. The recognition of God's presence in Christ is by faith, and proceeds from faith to faith. Man's freedom is not over-ridden. God's grace is pure grace, pure gift, and man can neither provide it nor be saved without it, but he can refuse it, and even, by unfaith, deny its existence, let alone its nature. Faith proceeds from faith to faith. Christ's healing work is first done by him by faith, and proclaimed by Christ, by faith, to be what it is. Though the uniqueness of the person and life of Christ means that the mode of his faith is not identical with ours, yet he exercises in his person the same God-given talent of faith, and resists the basic human temptation of unfaith. If Christ was

[1] Cf. the author's 'Judgement in Psychiatry', *Frontier*, Summer, 1961.

'one that hath been in all points tempted like as we are, yet without sin' (Heb. 4:15) then he was tempted to unfaith but was perfect in faith. His divinity fulfils his humanity and his perfect person embodies the perpetual courageous activity of faith, under perpetual temptation of unfaith, 'and in the execution of this obedience his divine dignity is not diminished but manifested'.[1] In faith Christ does the work of the Father, and in faith he proclaims them to be the works of the Father. Long before Peter makes his declaration of faith, Jesus has made his declaration of faith in the Father's presence in the healing miracles. Jesus first makes this declaration of faith on behalf of all men, and he must first do this in the humanity as well as in the divinity of his one person, in a concrete here and now situation. 'If I by the finger of God cast out devils, then doubtless the Kingdom of God is come upon you.' The disciples must do the same and 'Heal the sick and say unto them, The Kingdom of God is come nigh unto you.' Faith responds to faith, and so we read in the Gospel how the healing of the blind man of Bethsaida (Mk. 8:22–26) is followed by Peter's declaration 'Thou art the Christ' (Mk. 8:27–30). Jesus' faith, manifested in his healing and preaching, is necessary to Peter's declaration of faith; and Peter's recognition of the Kingdom of God present, really present, here and now in the blind man's healing, is necessary to the other apostles' faith, and through them to ours. So the remembrance of Christ's healing work is not just a remembrance and imitation of his philanthropic act. It is also a remembrance and repetition[2] of the faith in which he both did it and proclaimed its nature. Faith demands of faith 'Heal the sick and say unto them "Ye have seen the Christ".' Such faith is not, of course, either psychological insight into what can be achieved with the sick by techniques such as suggestion, or an optimistic opinion that if the blind man turns his expectations to God he will receive sight, but acceptance of Christ as Lord. So the response of Peter is the recognition of a new law and covenant, not a discovery or revelation of new laws of psycho-

[1] Mascall, E. L., op. cit., p. 52.
[2] 'Repetition' here must be subject to the same limitations as when it is used of the Holy Communion. Christ lives on, and the Church's repetition is more accurately described as a joining in, made possible by his incarnate work, the eternal offering of Christ.

dynamics. Peter, when he says 'Thou art the Christ', is not recognising and joining a faith cure group, but becoming the Church, and by that fact a member of a therapeutic community.

Christ was present as Saviour, healing the sick in Israel (Palestine) long ago, but he was only a Saviour for men in that healing work in so far as they saw him as such, and accepted him as such. His real presence as Saviour waited upon the faith of men. The concept of a person's real presence being dependent upon another person's response and not only on his physical location in space and time is a difficult one. For philosophical explanations we can only point to the Eucharist and the Church as similar to the sacrament of healing and suggest that Christ's real presence in these may be in similar modes; but the possibility of the real presence of one person depending upon another may perhaps be more easily visualised of recent years because of the trends of some philosophy and psychiatry.

> Personal being is essentially being in relation, not being in isolation. The first personal pronoun, has been removed from that lonely eminence it has occupied in the thinking of philosophers since Descartes, and the second has taken its place alongside it. The pattern of personal being is no longer conceived of as a circle with 'I' at the centre; it has become an ellipse with two foci, 'I and thou' . . . there can be no I without a Thou.'[1]

So Christ, in principle present in every man as Saviour, by his incarnate work, is actually present as Saviour in a few, but potentially present in all. Christ's healing-saving work is continued in its fulness only by faith. Only in faith can men obey the commission of Christ to heal the sick and declare the real presence of the Saviour. And only by faith can men respond to such preaching.

Jesus promised his disciples that they would do 'greater works than these' (Jn. 10:12) when he had gone to the Father and the Spirit had come to them. On that day, the prophecy of Joel 2:28 would be fulfilled, and the Spirit which had been upon Christ would be poured out upon all men. The day of Pentecost was considered by the early Church to be that day.

[1] Hendry, G. S., op. cit., p. 105.

When all are amazed on the day of Pentecost, and puzzled by the meaning of all that had happened, St Peter declares that God has now poured out his Spirit upon all flesh (Acts 2:14f). The result of this gift of the Spirit, we are told by the author of Acts, was repentance, baptism, fellowship, prayers, breaking of bread, sharing of possessions, and the working of many wonders and signs by the Apostles. These are the 'greater works'. The author of Acts immediately follows this description with the account of the healing of the lame man at the Temple gate (Acts 3). Jesus heals him through his power (name). Now 'in the name of' has a much stronger representative content than we usually ascribe to it. We are inclined to think of it like 'in the name of the law', where the arresting policeman states his authority. Even here the policeman is part of the law he represents and is empowered by it in the exercise of his duty. But in the New Testament usage this representative aspect is stronger. Peter doesn't say to the lame man just, 'I am authorised and empowered by Jesus Christ to tell you to stand up and walk.' When he says 'Walk in the name of Jesus Christ' he means 'Walk [live] within and in the power of Jesus Christ', for Hebraically 'to walk' is to live. Peter thus witnesses to this power within Jesus, in his words to the lame man (Acts 3:6) and to the witnesses of what has happened. Peter says: 'It isn't what you think. This man hasn't been healed either by our own power, or our own holiness, but faith in Christ's power has made this man whole. Therefore repent' (Acts 3:12–19).

This first healing of the Church has many lessons to teach us.

(a) The lame man represents and presents the sickness of the community, not only in his lameness, but in the whole set-up of his life. The bringing of the man daily to the Temple Gates and his maintenance by alms outside the Temple Gates, is the perfect example of community life lived at compromise, half-life, level. What should be tackled radically by patient and community, is only timidly dealt with by all concerned. The collusion[1] between the lame man, the com-

---

[1] This collusion is, psycho-dynamically speaking, a feature of all human relationship. The dominant mother is not dominant totally by coercion but always partly by consent of the child, and where the collusion is satisfactory to everybody the psychiatrist, but not the pastor, is out of a job. This collusion is what Erich Fromm attacks as 'egoism à deux'. Cf. *The Art of Loving*, Allen and Unwin, 1957.

munity, humane instincts, and religious observance (outside the Temple) is a perfect example of an unconscious conspiracy to adopt a half-life, which makes only restricted demands on all.

(b) Peter and John, as the Church, in (the name of) Christ recognise the need of the sick man. They do not disregard the fact that he is lame, and should be helped to be healed in the muscles and joints of his legs.

(c) They make the situation a 'crisis' situation for the man and the community. They state that the man must and can live in the power of Christ, at the same time joining themselves to the man (his right hand) and lifting him up. Thus Peter, having faith, already sees the situation in terms of salvation crisis, makes the crisis present by joining himself, and Christ in him, to the sick man, and lifting him up by his hand. This, together with Peter's preaching, makes it a salvation crisis for all the witnesses. It is the witnesses as much as the lame man, who are 'put on the spot' by this healing and preaching. Will they see the presence of Christ, or close their eyes to his presence? They must either repent, and receive the new refreshing (3:19) life, or be destroyed (3:23). None of them will ever be the same again.

(d) The result is that the Church (here Peter and John) begins to suffer (Acts 4:3) and many come to believe (4:4).

Here then, in their first detailed healing work, the Apostles obey the Lord's command to heal the sick and preach the Kingdom, and they do in Christ a remembrance of Christ. This is a true remembrance (ἀνάμνησις) in the biblical sense;[1] which is not merely an idea of something which is not really the thing itself but is a recalling of the thing itself. Thus Peter and John have done, at the gate of the Temple, a remembrance of what Christ did to other paralysed men (cf. Mk. 2) They were faithful in this as they were when they observed the Lord's command 'Do this in remembrance of me' by doing the Holy Communion. Thus what Peter and John have done at the Temple gate, is to make Christ present as Saviour, or perhaps we should say, they have by their faith consented that Christ might be really present

[1] For a full study, cf. M. Thurian, *The Eucharistic Memorial*, Lutterworth Press, 1960.

in this situation as Saviour, just as he was in his healing work before his Crucifixion. For, as Richardson points out,[1] 'the eucharistic remembrance is primarily a divine and not a human remembering', for εἰς τὴν ἐμὴν ἀνάμνησις means literally 'do it within my remembrance'. That is, it is Christ alive who is doing the remembering, and who is in Peter and John speaking and acting to the sick man, and in the sick man suffering for him and rising with him, and in 'all the people'[2] (v.9) at their time of judgment. There is at the gate of the Temple a real presence which brings and announces the day of salvation. Peter and John are not only copying Christ, nor only remembering him in the weak sense of the word, nor even only 'remembering' Christ in the stronger sense of the word, though they are doing all these things. Rather it is Christ who is remembering them, as God remembered the people of Israel, and saved them from the hands of their enemies, delivering them from bondage and the consequences of their sins. But just as God's remembrance in the Old Testament is his coming in Passover, both to save and to judge, so also Peter and John's work is an occasion of condemnation as well as deliverance. Men and women at the Temple gate were in the presence of God, in the terrible presence of love. By their response they judged themselves, some to enter into the fellowship of life and some to kill the prince of life, and cut themselves off from him who had come to be present as Saviour in their lives. 'He that believeth on him is not condemned; but he that believeth not is condemned already, because he hath not believed in the name of the only begotten Son of God' (Jn. 3:18).

One further point must now be developed about the healing of the lame man at the Gate called Beautiful. Point (d) included the statement that 'the result [of the healing] was that the Church began to suffer'. This illustrates a fact which so many people interested in spiritual healing find it difficult to accept. We have already mentioned that the healing work of Christ was a sin-bearing. When Christ, whose body the Church now is, touched the leper (Mk. 1:41) he identified himself with the sick-sinful man, and in Christ, in this wholeness (unity) with

---

[1] *An Introduction to New Testament Theology*, p. 368.

[2] 'All the people' (πᾶς ὁ λαός) reminds us again of healing as a public effective sign.

Christ, the man's leprosy is relieved. This is a union which has not magically made the suffering disappear, but synthetised it in a perfect wholeness which suffers it, and whose suffering manifests the glory[1] (i.e. reveals the Godhead).

The Son of Man who joins himself to the leper, the paralytic, the woman who is a sinner, the blind man, is the 'Son of Man who must suffer', but the 'must suffer' is not an accidental concomitant of the joining of himself in healing. It is a consequence. This is what we hinted, when we said that immediately Christ put out his hand to touch the leper he chose his Gethsemane. When love joined sin and suffering, its wholeness was not destroyed, for the wholeness is a wholeness which includes suffering. The sick man's faith, if faith is thought of as a deeply penetrating act of personal commitment to another person, consents to a union with the whole Christ. And in the continuance of that work today, the whole Body, to whom the faithful are joined, *suffers* in that joining.

The suffering of Christ is not a meaningless or insignificant by-product of either his healing work or his whole works, but is the very keynote, the very mark, the very fruit, of his perfect obedience. The author of Hebrews states plainly that God 'made Christ perfect *through* suffering' (2:10). The healings of the Gospels are therefore unions of man with Man, in which the sick man joins in a wholeness which bears his suffering. The burden of cosmic and communal sin, presented in the paralytic's withered arm, and the leper's skin, is joined to Christ. But because the healed man is in personal communion with Christ (faith is consent to such a union), the sick man both slips off sin-disease, gaining useful limbs or clean skin, and at the same time enters, with Christ, into a greater burden. Those modern and ancient Gnostics, who see perfect faith in Christ as necessitating perfect freedom from suffering, must not only set aside the bloody and exhausted Christ on the cross, but Christ's repeated statements that faith in him means sharing in his suffering—victorious suffering, manifesting glory, but still

---

[1] Bearing in mind St John's affirmation that the crucifixion is the lifting up of the Son of Man in his glorification. But it is God's love in Christ, loving men even when it involves suffering unto death which is glorious, and not suffering considered as an activity in itself. The suffering of Christ is never chosen by him for itself. Men may be made martyrs; they cannot choose to be true martyrs.

6

suffering. Here indeed is a mystery which is proclaimed in the life of Christ. He who would save his life must lose it. He who would be made whole must suffer as he joins the suffering of man in Christ.

What Christ did when he stretched forth his hand to the leper he offers himself to continue in Peter and John, by their faith permitting him to be in them at the gate of the Temple. He stretches forth his hand to the lame man and lifts him into union with himself. Here and now the man is joined to the Church, and with them he enters (v. 8) into the Temple. Now in 'the whole Christ' the lame man shares in their walking into the Temple, and their praising God. No doubt too he shares in the consequences for the Church, of the Church's ministry to him, and these consequences are both success (Acts 4:4) and suffering (4:3). Christ, having identified himself in his earthly life with all men, and particularly with the weak, the deprived, the sick, and his apostles, promises that he *will continue* to be in the weak, the sick, the deprived, and his apostles.

It is noteworthy that Christ's pronouncements upon his organic unity with man, which Mersch in his book *The Whole Christ*[1] shows tradition to have used in building the doctrines of the Mystical Body, refer more to sufferers than to apostles. There is a sense in which the Mystical Body is not the ecclesiastical apostolic congregation that we call the Church, but the mystical body of suffering men and women. Those who would join the Mystical Body must have communion with a sufferer. Not only in the consecrated elements, not only in the Church, but also in the sufferer does faith know the real presence and by communion with each partake of the spiritual Christ.

In the early Church, then, the corporate effective signs of the Gospel healings are continued. The Church in Christ, Christ in his Church, the whole Christ, Peter and John, do an 'anamnesis'. What happens?

(*a*) Christ stretches out his hand and has communion with the sickness and sinfulness of men and women here 'presenting' in the lame man.

(*b*) The stretching out to heal is done in the Church, in Christ,

---

[1] Mersch ,E., trans. J. R. Kelly, 1949, Dennis Dobson.

by faith and obedience, for the Father, just as Christ not only did good works (others had done this), but did them as a Saviour who had been sent.

(c) At the same time the Church, Peter and John, Christ in the Church, verbally proclaimed Christ's presence. 'Thou hast both seen him, and it is he that talketh with you.' In me on Ward A bringing you a cup of water. In him injecting penicillin in Ward B.

(d) The healing work, the presence of God in power, is both a declaration and implementation of God's making himself present in power and judgment. Peter and John in Christ really DO the healing. It isn't just a sign or symbol in the weak meaning of the words, just a sermon make-believe. They do an effective sign which brings in what it declares.

(e) The consequence of this healing work done by Christ-in-Peter and John-in-the-Church, is that all the witnesses are judged. God has visited his people once again, making himself once more of no reputation, and in his Body the Church, in the form of a servant, has joined himself to a cripple. God is manifesting his glory once again, and here is another *shekhinah* in a temple, in a beggar outside the gates. And, as Peter proceeds to point out, this is the day of judgment for all the witnesses.

(f) As a result of this, Christ offers wholeness to men; some accept, but share in him the result, which is another step towards Jerusalem where he, and they in him, will both suffer and be glorified. Christ's healing work in the Church, like his healing work in his earthly Ministry, are corporate effective signs. They announce and bring to the community salvation and judgment.

(g) Some reject the corporate effective signs and deny Christ, and they are judged already.

CHAPTER 7

HOLY COMMUNION IN THE CUP OF COLD WATER AND THE CUP OF BLESSING

IT WILL HAVE BEEN noticed how we have used words in relation to the healing work of Christ and the early Church, which are ordinarily used by theologians in the discussion of Holy Communion. The employment of such terms has been deliberate. Here are some of the approximations between Holy Communion and merciful healing acts done in and by Christ, which have thus been intimated:

1. *The Dominical command*
'Do this'   'Heal the sick and say . . .'

2. *The remembrance of what was uniquely done*
The remembrance of the   The remembrance of the
whole life offered on the Cross   whole life offered to the sick
                                                    and suffering

3. *The real presence*
'This is my body'   'Ye did it unto me'
'This is my blood'   'Whosoever receiveth . . .
                                                    receiveth me'

4. *The eschatological reference*
The Great Supper   The healing of all nations.

5. *The sacrifice*
The offertory: the congrega-   The sick visitor offers him-
tion offer themselves and their   self in the Church in Christ
everyday lives in Christ with   in sacrificial acts of service
Christ

74

6. *They give grace to those who receive them rightly*

Sanctification, though still sinners;	Healing, yet suffering remains;
Not just an imputation;	Not just an imputation;
Even now, but not yet	Even now, but not yet

We have used this language of sacramental theology because we intend to argue that in fact we are dealing with two closely related sacraments, ultimately inseparable because they stem from one Incarnate Lord. Yet they are two separate sacraments, necessarily done in different ways and times and places, by the same necessity which distinguished a healing miracle in Galilee from the crucifixion outside the walls of Jerusalem; a glorious necessity, because it exhibited the fullness of the work of God in Christ. The communion with God, in the hand that touches the leper, is at one with the communion with God in the hand that breaks the bread in the Upper Room.

We shall then proceed to show in more detail the close similarities between the healing ministry and the saving death of Christ on the one hand, and the sacrament of healing and the sacrament of Holy Communion on the other. We do this for two reasons. First, because we wish to communicate some of the corporate aspects of each to the other, and second, because the actual parish situation today demands some such communication between the Holy Communion in the Church building and the work for the sick and suffering in the parish boundaries. But though we use terms of sacramental theology to make this communication, we are aware that this is only one of several channels open to us. One basic defect of theology today is, as Hendry claims in *The Gospel of the Incarnation*, the fragmentation of the Gospel. This leads to fragmentary theologies, which help to initiate and maintain not only Church disunity, but fragmentation of the life and work of every Church. One way of combating this fragmentation is to remember at all times that Christ's healing life is the same life that was incarnate in the womb of Mary, and that was given on the Cross. We must beware, for example, of deriving a theology of Baptism from Christ's Baptism, a theology of work and healing from Christ's carpentry and healing, and a theology of the Holy

Communion from the Upper Room and Calvary. The theology of each and all must come from the understanding of each and all. We could, as an alternative or supplementary method, draw close comparisons between the Word in the healing miracles and the Word in the pulpit, insisting on a Real Presence in each, and with great profit. But we must limit the task, and the present Liturgical Movement in all communions suggests that discussion of the relation between Holy Communion and the ministry to the sick may be most acceptable and profitable. Whilst on first impressions this may be uncongenial to those Christians who take a 'low' view of the sacraments, it may in fact prove most offensive to those who are at home with a 'high' view of the sacraments, but tend to have a 'low' view of the laity.

The sacraments of Christ are so closely associated in the minds of men and women with their operation by an ordained ministry, that the absence of an ordained minister, at any rate as we visualise one, from merciful and healing acts, will appear at first glance to invalidate them as sacraments. We shall meet this objection by maintaining that the ministry to the sick and suffering is performed by the priesthood of all believers, through those who have been called to this ministry, as others have been called to the ministry of the sacrament of Holy Communion. These two sacraments are performed by two different ministries and representatives (in the strong sense) of the priesthood of all believers.[1] Different gifts are exercised in different callings 'set in the Church' (1 Cor. 12:28). This recognition of one priesthood of all believers, but diverse ministries, in no way necessitates a depreciation of either priesthood or sacrament. This is not to deny that it has frequently, or even usually, been used for this purpose in the past, and in the Reformation in particular. But the priesthood of all believers is a positive doctrine. Priesthood of all believers does not mean 'the priesthood of no believers whatsoever' or 'the non-priesthood of all believers'.[2] The minister who celebrates the Holy Communion

[1] Note that the priesthood of all believers has an 'oscillation' between an individualistic aspect and a corporate aspect. Every single Christian is a priest, yet any Christian is a priest only in so far as he participates in, and so can be a representative of the corporate priesthood, the people of God. This corporate aspect is well expounded in C. Eastwood, *The Priesthood of All Believers*, Epworth, 1960.
[2] Manson, T. W., *Ministry and Priesthood: Christ's and Ours*, Epworth, 1958, p. 40.

as representative of the priestly people has been called by God and the local congregation to a special honour and humility. The Christian doctor, nurse, probation officer, or sick visitor has been called by God and the local congregation to a special honour and humility. Both are to celebrate a communion of Christ with his whole Body. 'Do this in remembrance of me' and also 'Do *this* in remembrance of me.'

The Church must join in the eternal offering by Christ of his life. The laity of the Church are priests who both individually and in the Church offer Christ in the Church to the world, to his whole Body. All can do this, but some are called by God and the congregation to special ministries. In these they do and speak an *anamnesis* (remembrance), in which the Church-in-Christ offers their lives in a remembrance and thanksgiving and oblation. When the person is called and commissioned to do this in Holy Communion we call him a minister of religion. When the person is called and commissioned to do this to the sick we call him a Christian doctor or nurse or by a similar title.

We must now turn to another difficulty, which concerns not the celebrant of the sacrament of the ministry to the sick and the concept of priesthood, but the question of set form and set words describing and effecting what is being done. In traditional terms a sacrament involves the *sacramentum tantum* (sacrament alone) which is the outward visible activity, such as the giving of bread and wine in the Eucharist or the use of water in Baptism. Christ through his ministers makes the *res et sacramentum* (reality and sacrament) and the result is the *res tantum* (reality alone), which is the union of Christ with the participants. Now in so far as merciful acts in the ministry to the sick are necessarily diverse in their character, it may be argued that recognised form embodying the sacrament is impossible; but a similar diversity characterised Christ's healing works, though they translated one consistent human activity, namely, his self-sacrificing compassion for others. And again, if, together with the greater part of Christendom we accept marriage as a sacrament, then we have the same problems of defining what is the form. The answer is given usually in terms of the love between Christ and his Church, and it is suggested that the love of husband and wife is made in the sacrament a sacramental memorial of this. But Christ's love for the Church is translated into diverse actions and so is the love of husband and wife. There is then no unanswerable objection over the matter of 'form'.

Another difficulty is the absence, at the time of the giving of the cup of cold water, of set words pronouncing what is being done. For words which proclaim the connection between the sign and the reality signified are usually considered necessary in a sacrament, though sometimes there is a disagreement as to what in fact is signified, and/or what are the correct words. In the case of the sacrament of mercy there are dominical words to hand, such as, 'The Kingdom of God is come nigh unto you', 'Ye did it unto me', or 'Receiveth me'. Thus some suitable form of words could be adopted, as for example, 'We give and receive this cup of cold water in remembrance of Christ's promises, that he by faith may be present in us, and we in him'; but formally to pronounce these words at each act of mercy is clearly impossible, and this may appear to make a true sacrament of mercy impossible. Two facts, however, suggest that this may not be a real obstacle. The first is that Christ himself, in the merciful acts and healing works with which he instituted the sacrament of mercy, did not invariably interpret with words the effective signs at the moment of their accomplishment. Certainly he both acts and proclaims the nature of the reality in which the witnesses have participated. The action and the words of the sacrament of mercy are both there in the New Testament, as clearly as for Baptism and the Eucharist, when Christ commands, 'Heal the sick and say unto them, The Kingdom of God is come nigh unto you', but the Gospels do not suggest that Christ's merciful works and his proclamation of what he is doing proceeded in strict alternation. The second fact is that if we acknowledge marriage as a sacrament, then we already have a sacrament in which there is a separation between the time of its formal and public verbal proclamation, and its lifelong continuance in private by the laity. Thus the impossibility of invariably pronouncing set words at the time of the giving of the cup of cold water, does not necessarily disqualify it from being accepted as a sacrament, for the public pronouncements of the

Church and of the doers of the acts of mercy, that these same acts are works of Christ, supplies the necessary form.

There are, then, some good grounds for claiming recognition for a sacrament of mercy. The New Testament evidence of its institution by Christ bears comparison with Baptism and the Eucharist and far exceeds that for some of the five other sacraments recognised by the Roman Catholic and Eastern Orthodox Churches. The absence of dominical precision in the institution of this sacrament cannot be a serious obstacle to those who hold the seven, whilst the strength of the evidence may give pause to those who recognise only the two.

At this point it seems wise to deal with three of the many possible misapprehensions:

(a) *That it is being claimed that any merciful act is a Christian sacrament.*

This is not so. Whilst it is true that in one very important passage in which Christ identifies himself with the sufferer (Matt. 25:31 ff) he does not say that the deeds were done in his name, in all the other passages the phrase 'in my name' is prominent. Therefore whilst there is no need to draw a sharp border-line between a merciful act which is deliberately and consciously done by a Christian in the power and name of Christ, and one done by a pagan in a spirit of compassion, it serves no purpose to suggest that they are indistinguishable. As has so often been pointed out, it is impossible to say when a boy becomes a man, but quite clear that there is a difference between them. Both wisdom and humility, especially Matt. 25:31 ff and 7:21–23 will, however, suggest that we use these distinctions to look to our priesthood and its responsibilities and not to confine Christ's presence to the ecclesiastical sacraments.

(b) *That it is being suggested that the sacrament of mercy (healings) renders the Holy Communion less precious or even redundant*

We have tried to deal briefly with the question why, if healing acts are those ordered and demonstrated by Christ, it is necessary for the Christian worker in medicine and allied fields, to make any other specific witness, i.e. to *speak* of Christ. In doing so we have claimed that the Christian in the Church, and the

Church in the Christian, is required to make of the healing situation a sacrament. Now it may be suggested that if this is done there is no need for Holy Communion. The first and the last answer to this is, of course, that the same Lord who bids us do one, bids us do the other. It is one of our human frailties that so often we can raise enthusiasm in ourselves and in others for one aspect of the whole Christ only by belittling another aspect. To this human sin is added the fact that we cannot be in two places at once, and there are only twenty-four hours in the day, so that enthusiasm for one thing may mean neglect of another. But if we think in terms of a hierarchy of Christian sacraments and of one basic one holding all others on top we have abandoned the organic models for which we have pleaded. The perfect body of the whole Christ is not the result of perfecting one part and then spreading the perfection,[1] for there is no such thing as either local disease or local perfection. Just as schism weakens not one part but every part of the Church, so neglect of one aspect of the Christian life weakens all. Thus for example, Holy Communion and what we call the Christian sacrament of mercy and healing, either thrive together or not at all. Failure to obey the Lord's commission to go to the sick means that many whom the Lord has bidden us bring to his feast have not even received an invitation. How can Christ do a remembrance of himself in his body, the Church, if his body the Church has not and will not obediently and faithfully offer its communion to the sick? Not only by taking the elements to the sick, but by taking themselves joined to Christ in Communion, and communicating with the sick and thus sharing their suffering, can the seats at the Lord's Supper be filled. The Holy Communion and the sacrament of healing are parts of one body, and there can be no question of competition between them.

(c) *That it is being suggested that Christ limits his coming to men to heal, and to save, to either Holy Communion, or to merciful and healing acts, or to any other listed situations*

As is well known, the New Testament contains much which

---

[1] Naturally this does not apply where Christ is described as the head of the body in the anatomical sense.

will support both those who believe that only an elect few are to be saved, and those who believe that God's love will not rest until every sheep is in his fold. Our Lord himself spent most of his time with a small band whom he had called and yet made it quite clear that his mission and theirs was to go out to those who were most in need. This double action of Christ of election for universalism runs through the New Testament: Christ in the Church confronting and judging the world, Christ in the world confronting and judging the Church. Those who feel that a 'High' view of the Church involves a kind of bilateral trade agreement between Christ and the Church in which both agree to have no other dealings elsewhere, will wish to confine Christ's healing and saving work to authorised and properly conducted work done by the authorised Church. Those who, whilst in no way disputing that the Church has been given specific duties and specific authority which embrace all God's work, do not believe that the Church is thereby made sole agents, will see Christ not only in the sufferer but also in the non-Christian man of mercy. Just as the exaltation of grace does not require a doctrine of total human depravity,[1] so the belief that Christ specifically charged and authorised his disciples to continue his work of healing does not require that Christ will not be present at healing except through the visible Church.

The Church's ministry of healing is thus a sacrament of the real presence of Christ. We must now ask in what modes he is present. Christ is present in his creation as originator and sustainer. St Paul writes of Christ in Colossians: 'For by him were all things created, that are in heaven, that are visible, that are invisible.' In all creation we can see by reason and revelation God's presence, essence, and power, but he is present whether we recognise and acknowledge it or not. Moreover, it can be argued that Christ is present not only as Creator, but also as re-creator. He came down from Heaven to lift up not only the mind and emotions of Man, but his whole nature, for he was made flesh. And that flesh springs from the inorganic dust and

---

[1] Mascall, E. L., 'There is it seems to me, an all too common assumption in present-day theology that, if X is greater than Y, the necessary consequence is that Y must be very small . . . as if however an exalted view of nature we take (even of fallen nature) there were not unlimited room for grace above it.'

returns to inorganic through a whole complexity of natural
and biological mechanisms. The human frame is, we are told
by popular scientists, turned over once every seven years. As
Adam's disobedience is followed not only by human fall but by
disorders of nature, so Christ by his work as the Second Adam
has reordered the cosmic disorder, though the whole creation still
groans. What he has already done in principle becomes actual
in the work of the pharmaceutical chemist, the agricultural
officer, and the water preservation board. In his baptism the
Christian descends with Christ into the watery waste and void,
the chaotic deep ruled by the Leviathan, ancient symbol of
Chaos, to rise with him already in principle a research worker,
a dam builder, or a malarial control officer. Baptism is in this
sense the first healing sacrament of the Church, for it incor-
porates men and women into a therapeutic community which
is healing the broken unity of Man and Nature. Christ is
present then in the clinical event firstly as creator and secondly
as re-creator of the world.

The third mode in which we see Christ's presence in the
clinical event is in the suffering-mercy-healing situation where
he is present as reconciler of man with man and man with God.
He is present in each and all of these situations by his Incarnation, for he was made not only a man, but also he was made
Man.

The sacrament of the cup of cold water is public, communal,
social, not only in the weak sense of being not done privately or
secretly, but in the strong sense of the word. Not a mere spect-
acle, a thing to be gazed upon, not a play or an opera. They are
communal in that they are done in the community and to the
community, for the healed man presents and represents their
sickness-sinful situation, so that for the observers to see the
man's predicament in terms of sin and judgment, and to accept
the Christ as Saviour into that man's situation, is to make the
same act of repentance and acceptance of salvation for themselves. Thus, the saving faith of the patient within the clinical
event offers salvation to other participant observers. For faith
proceeds from faith. Peter responds to the clinical event of the
giving of sight to blind Bartimeus by permitting the Lord the
Spirit to open his eyes and see the real presence. He says:

'Thou art the Christ of that man and of me.' As the nurse's witness to the real presence in the clinical event offers salvation to all around the sick-bed, so Peter's verbal witness was essential to the apostles' and through them to our salvation. For faith is not an assent to a proposition, nor a withdrawal of reason, but a committal of the reasonable self to a relationship with God through Christ, so that the healing works of Christ are effective signs, instituted by him, offering a particular form of union with him which gives grace to those who receive it rightly.

The conception of a sacrament as instituting a saving relationship with men and God through Christ[1] is most welcome at a time when in medicine the healing power of loving relationships is being stressed. When it is taught in the medical schools that the infant needs a constant tender love as it needs adequate milk. When the treatment of neurotic, psychosomatic, and psychopathic traits is centred on therapeutic techniques of acceptance and understanding, in the establishment of an empathy in which the transference situation can be revealed and interpreted. This helps us to understand something of the way in which God has accomplished his work of sending his son to save us, and to bridge the gap between the ancient historical act and the present salvation of men. By these psychological concepts we can get some insight, never forgetting it is only an analogy, of how the healing, saving presence can continue today in the sacraments of the Eucharist and the cup of cold water.

A remembrance of an inter-personal event is not a mere cerebral activity separable from one's being, as when we remember twice two is four, but is a recapitulation of that event, a reparticipation in it. As Max Thurian details in his study of *The Eucharistic Memorial*, the Jews by their recital of God's mighty acts participate again with their forefathers, as when they remember the Exodus in their Passover. Jesus at the Last Supper may have said, 'Blessed art thou, O Lord, our God, King of the earth, who hast given to thy people Israel this season for festivity and joy in a memorial.' Analogous to this memorial in Judaism is the memorial or remembrance in psychiatric theory and practice. The remembrance of infantile experiences is capable of healing only when it is no mere

[1] See p. 88, footnote.

impersonal act but is a renewal, a reliving of those past experiences. Psychotherapy is planned so that such experiences can be recapitulated and redeemed within the transference situation. A twentieth-century triumph of science foreshadowed by Irenaeus in his recapitulation theory of the Atonement in the second century! Now the remembrance of Christ in the sacraments is not only the remembrance of his passion and death, but of the whole life offered, for, as we have been reminded of recent years, the sacrifice of blood in Semitic thought is the sacrifice not of a death, but of a life. So then the remembrance of Christ's healing works is a sacramental act, an effective sign which establishes a union between the participants and God. They are given to be sacraments of unity, and therefore healing and saving acts, between Christ and men. For the remembrance of boundless love and forgiveness is a participation in actuality in what has already taken place in principle. To be in the presence of Christ is to be in the presence of a love beside which the therapist's is pale.

What divides a sacrament from a no-sacrament is that there is in a sacrament an intention, a general intention, though not necessarily thought or spoken at the precise time, to do what Christ commanded us to do in the remembrance of him, in the form of a sacrificial act of love joining the participants to each other and to Christ. The objectivity of the sacrament resides firstly in the fact that what is remembered is a historical fact which we could not and did not do, but was done by God in Christ, and secondly in that it is the Lord the Spirit which prompts and empowers us to make the remembrance. The subjectivity of the sacrament resides in the fact that only the free person can do a full remembrance in the sense of accepting it into his being in the here and now. There is inspiration of loving acts by the Spirit, as there is of biblical writings, but in both cases it is not mechanical inspiration contemptuous of free will. This idea of a remembrance as a personal saving commitment may be partially illuminated by an example from psychiatry. It is generally accepted that there are different levels of recall of past events, with different therapeutic efficiencies. The doctor may, for example, know from outside sources of a traumatic event in the life of the patient which is the key to his present sickness, but the mere bringing it to mind is unlikely to be effective. The patient may say to the doctor, that he accepts the proposition 'I was shut in the wood shed', as he might say to an instructing priest 'I accept the proposition, Jesus Christ is my Saviour', but this formal acceptance is unlikely to bring relief. More likely to bring relief in some cases is an abreaction under, say, ether or pentothal, in which the patient, perhaps prompted by the word of the doctor, recalls and relives with emotion the traumatic experience, and goes again through the anguish and bloody sweat of the wood shed, or the burning bomber, or the prison camp. But this is not enough, for like the conversion experience under mass-meeting circumstances it has to be brought closer to the real world. What was relived under ether has to be relived in the relationship with the doctor, in the transference situation. It is the commital of the whole life of the patient, including the traumatic experience, to a particular form of union with the therapist where it may be recapitulated within the love and acceptance of the therapist that is the saving remembrance. So too, a faithful remembrance of Christ's healing work is a personal committal to a union with Christ, a re-entry into the love and compassion which shook the sick long ago. Evangelical witness makes the clinical event a saving event, a sacrament.

This is illustrated by the story of the healing of the ten lepers in Luke 17. All were cleansed ($\dot{\varepsilon}\varkappa a\theta a\varrho i\sigma\theta\eta\sigma a\nu$), but one saw he was healed ($i\dot{a}\theta\eta$) and turned back and offered thanks ($\varepsilon\dot{v}\chi a\varrho\iota\sigma\tau o\tilde{\omega}\nu$), and he was saved ($\sigma\dot{\varepsilon}\sigma\omega\varkappa\dot{\varepsilon}\nu$). 'Saved' is the New Testament word for the entry into the New Covenant relationship of sonship made possible by Christ. The clinical event has become for the tenth leper a saving event. We must here make a very brief reference to the word '$\sigma\dot{\varepsilon}\sigma\omega\varkappa\dot{\varepsilon}\nu$' translated here 'made whole'. This wholeness is the entering into a relationship with God of sonship through Christ. It is neither cleansing nor healing, nor yet a kind of Greek *harmonia* of mind, body, and spirit, symbolised by Greek sculpture, an Apollo or a Venus. It is not Greek but Hebrew and it is a 'day of the Lord' word, describing the blessed state of those who are welcomed to the fold. This is what the word means in the Old Testament, this is what it means in the New Testament. There is a harmony there, but it is the harmony of self-sacrificing love, and the symbol is not the Greek Apollo, but the bloody, exhausted, twisted, and ugly body of Christ upon the Cross. The tenth leper has not been made, to use modern language, a balanced personality, the kind of person who cannot be faulted by physical or psychological examination, a little psychiatrist. He has been made one with Christ, a little Christ, a Christian. This salvation is by his faith committing himself on his knees in a Eucharist to God in Christ in the clinical event.

The tenth leper teaches us how the Christian in the Church, and the Church in the Christian, by their word of oblation and thanks about the clinical event changes the clinical situation, deepens the diagnosis, and effects salvation. The making whole is preceded by the acceptance of his situation of sickness and healing as one that has its meaning in a relationship with God. This is the truth in the mistaken idea that a person is sick because of sin, and can get well only if he confesses his sin. The acceptance of the sickness as a defect of relationship with God is not just a religious truth which is irrelevant to the clinical situation, but is part of the diagnosis and therefore changes the plan of therapy. There is a new level of diagnosis which is analogous to the recognition that the ulcer in a man's stomach is a function not only of the structure of his gastric mucosa, or the function of his acid juices, but of his relationship with his wife, father, and mother. The physician in principle can effect a radical cure of the complaint only if he cures the relationships. In fact, however, he may confine himself to the local lesion. The making of the clinical event a salvation event is to diagnose it as a predicament of wrong relations between man and man, and man and God. That the connecting-links are most tenuous and resistant to investigation and therapy does not detract from this truth.

The word of God in the preaching of the Church to the clinical event to make of it a sacrament is thus diagnostic as well as potentially therapeutic. It is also very toxic. The word of God in Christ, and in his healing miracles brought judgment, because men and women confronted with love, rejected it and were judged already. It is a toxic, lethal drug in this respect, because as the spirit of truth, he threatens psychosomatic and psychoneurotic defences, giving the patient an awful glimpse of the truth from which his defences protect him. As neurotic anxiety may react to truth by a strengthening of the defences and a rejection of the therapist, so existential anxiety, unfaith, reacts to the Word by a strengthening of the defences and rejection of Christ and his priests. Not only bad religion, but good religion, good priests, good Christ, are rejected by men who are thus judged already and become more sick. Preaching Christ at the clinical event, the sacrament, produces not only salvation crisis but judgment crisis. If Christ had been content to do wonders, he would not have been crucified. It is when he says of the clinical events, his healings, that in them the salvation events promised by Isaiah have been fulfilled, that the crowd throw him out of the synagogue, reject him, and later crucify him. The word of God is diagnostic, therapeutic and, received unworthily, very toxic. This, incidentally, raises grave problems for the relationship of hospital chaplains with medical staff and of parish priests with general practitioners. As the psychiatrist has to decide with the physician whether to attempt a radical cure at the risk of the patient rejecting it and becoming more sick, so the chaplain or parish priest cannot both bring the sick man into a remembrance of Christ and run no risk of making him worse. Pastoral skill and psycho-dynamic insight cannot resolve this dilemma, for even the love of Christ which was perfect brought judgment, as does the real presence of God at all times.

We have digressed from our main theme, the sacrament of mercy and healing. The form is the clinical event, the words dominical. The priest is the lay ministry within the priesthood of all believers, the effect a union of love and service. What are the social limits? Where does the agnostic, the careless, the Hindu or Moslem come in? Most acceptable definitions of sacraments restrict their efficacy to the society of the Church, so that even the wonderful insight of the Mystical Body is at once constricted by identifying it with the Church. The tendency is to think of the Church as a privileged elect which grants full membership only under certain conditions and confines full benefit to those members. There are, of course, people outside peering through the windows and sniffing the cooking odours and collecting the left-overs. The sacrament of the cup of cold water, however, threatens this confined society. The ubiquity of merciful acts inspired in the hearts of men by the Lord the Spirit is obvious. These acts can, by the word of God, be made salvation events, so that the pagan social worker or surgeon may provide the form, as the bread or wine, and the Christian witness the word at quite another time and place. Together they make one sacrament which offers salvation to both Christian and non-Christian about the clinical event. This universalistic aspect of the cup of cold water, which if admitted as a sacrament would modify the concept of all sacraments, is also based upon the New Testament evidence of its ubiquity. In Matt. 25, nations are saved because of what they did to Christ, though they never knew his name. In Mk. 10, when John asks about the unauthorised man who was healing in Christ's power he is answered not only directly, but perhaps also by the institution immediately afterwards of the sacrament of the cup of cold water. We might therefore replace the words 'Christ's Mystical Body, the Church' in Professor Leerning's definition,[1] by something which includes the Church but is much wider socially. Perhaps 'Christ's whole body' or 'the fullness [pleroma] of Christ' would be satisfactory. The Church then becomes an essential, but not necessarily the central part of the sacrament, which is 'an effective sign of a particular form of union of God in Christ with the fullness of Christ, which gives wholeness to those who receive it rightly'. In this definition the compassionate work of men and women, nurse, porter, surgeon and almoner and priest, about the clinical event, becomes the means of salvation in Christ for them, the patients, the relatives, and the local community and the local Church. The Church is fed in this sacrament by the world, as the world by the Church.

We may conclude by saying that the healing situation is one in which the Church is directly commanded by the Lord to continue in him his earthly ministry of healing and proclaiming the rule of God. The Church is to declare and allow to be present the Saviour who is Christ the Lord. To do this they must, as Christ did, join themselves to sinners and sufferers and

---

[1] Cf. Professor B. Leeming's proposed definition of a sacrament as 'An effective sign instituted by Christ, of a particular form of union with his Mystical Body, the Church, which gives grace to those who receive it rightly', in his book *Principles of Sacramental Theology*, Longmans, 1956, p. 10.

be bruised with their afflictions. The joining of Christ in his
Church to the sick man means that both the sick man and the
Church enter into a larger unit, a larger wholeness in which
there is a common poverty-richness, a common penicillin-
absence of penicillin, a common faith-absence of faith, a
common suffering-absence of suffering. All things are shared.
The sin and the disease which mankind presents in one individual patient is declared common and borne by the Church.
For the Christian sacrament of ministering to the sick, like all
other Christian sacraments, is a sacrament of unity. They are
effective signs of unity between God and Man, and between
man and man. As effective signs they do and bring in what they
advertise. They declare and make visible and present the
mystical union of God in Christ with his Church and the
sufferer. They answer the command of Christ— be what you
are, sons of God and brothers, members of one another. So it is,
because the Holy Communion of the local church and the
Christian sacrament of ministering to the sick are both parts of
the same declaration of communion with Christ and the local
community, that the task of taking Christ in the Church to the
sick is no optional extra for the Church, not even a *'bene esse,'*
but an *'esse'*. The Christian sacrament of ministering to the sick
is a sacrament of unity in which the local community is made
whole-in-Christ.

CHAPTER 8

CORPORATE ASPECTS OF HUMAN 'WHOLENESS' IN RECENT BIBLICAL AND MEDICAL THOUGHT

THE PHRASE OF John Donne, 'No man is an island unto himself', has been much quoted of recent years. Recoiling from the excessive individualism of the nineteenth century, this midtwentieth century has re-discovered that man is a social being, whose personality can thrive only within a satisfactory communion with others. The ideal man is no longer thought of as one who controls within his person a variety of conflicting forces, called instincts, to produce a productive whole. He is one who, from the cradle to the grave, makes satisfactory relations with other people. This recoil is so sharp that there seems a danger that men and women will be rated only according to the frequency of their mutually satisfactory encounters with each other. In its most extreme form it sometimes appears that a den of thieves would score more marks than Christ, whose behaviour antagonised and separated him off from all men. However, despite the dangers of exaggeration, there has no doubt been a rediscovery of importance. Health and wholeness are now realised to be wider than the individual, and it is realised that there can be no perfect wholeness except within a perfectly whole society.

A consistent theme in recent writings about the ministry to the sick is the close relation between healing and wholeness. The writers all repeat that the Authorised Version, in several of the accounts of Christ's healing works, translates σέσωκέν as 'made whole', and that it is elsewhere translated as 'saved'. From this indisputable fact it is then argued that Christ's healings were not a now outmoded type of treatment, resulting only in the removal of symptoms, but a twentieth-century total healing of the whole man. Christ was then the forerunner of the modern physician, for modern medical opinion stresses the absolute necessity of dealing with the entire personality. Thus, it is argued, Christ's concept of healing and the concept of enlightened doctors today are identical. The next step in this way of thought is to declare that the doctor and the pastor are engaged upon the same task. The pastor's work is 'to save' (σώζειν) men and women, and this is to 'make them whole' (σώζειν). The psychiatrist, as he treats mind and body, the sexual, economic, artistic, social, religious, and all other needs of his patients, is directing his energies to 'make whole' and thus 'to save'.

There is much truth in the above argument, and it is based upon an important observation in the New Testament. It could lead to further valuable lessons for Church and medicine, for it could encourage medicine and theology to seek a rich and mutually acceptable philosophy of man drawn from the treasures of the two disciplines. In fact, however, the usual result is that recent concepts of medicine and psychiatry are imposed upon theology, and little or nothing taken in return—a kind of 'dark ages' in reverse. This is made possible by a loss of theological nerve by Christians, so complete that most of those who capitulate are blissfully unaware of what has happened. So the Christian philosophy of man, and therefore of 'health', is blown about by every change of wind in philosophy, psychiatry, and medicine, because there is no serious concern for 'the faith once delivered' and still accessible through biblical study and Christian doctrine. The end-result is fashionable, modern Christian attitudes, when what is required is contemporary Christian prophecy.

In this chapter we shall examine the phrase 'thy faith has made thee whole' (Ἡ πίστις σου σέσωκέν σε) in the hope that the Bible will speak to us in this generation. We shall study the various Greek words used to describe 'heal', 'cure', 'cleanse', 'make whole', and 'save'. We shall presuppose that these words do *not* reveal a conscious or unconscious classification, by Christ or the evangelists, of the various clinical events into different medically orientated aetiologies, therapies, or results. This presupposition is based upon the fact that only the strongest evidence would justify the anachronism of holding that when the Gospel makers chose the particular words used to describe the healings, they had medical classifications at the centre, or even perhaps at the periphery, of their minds. What was at the centre of their minds was the preaching of the Gospel and the recording of the life of Jesus in their life-situation. The events deposited in the Gospel are real events, not ones invented by the later Church. But the Gospel and doctrinal shape into which that deposit was moulded was largely determined by the needs of the struggling early Church.

During the thirty to sixty years between Christ's death and the solidification of the Gospels, the Church was preaching, teaching, living, worshipping, and fighting. In that life the words and works of Christ were recalled to give authority to decisions, to illuminate problems, to discountenance enemies, and to encourage and instruct catechumens. Central in this life of the early Church was the dispute with Judaism without and within. In this battle, the healing miracles are part of the Church's central armament. When, for example, there is mention of priests in the healing of the lepers, the writers are not concerned with the relation between doctors and pastors. They are concerned with problems such as whether a baptised Jew should still offer sacrifices at the Temple. It is because of this importance of problems of ceremonial uncleanness that there are frequent references to Christ's 'cleansing' of the lepers. The prominence of the healing works in the Gospel is due in large part to the crucial importance for the early Church of the theology of Baptism. What happens to men and women when they are baptised and become Christians? What shall they do about their previous Jewish practices? Shall they eat with Gentile Christians? Shall they require Gentile Christians to keep the laws about cleanness?

The key to the selection, shape, and choice of words of the healing miracles is the life-situation of the early Church, and in particular the need for instruction of catechumens for Baptism. For this reason, any discussion which neglects this aspect is seriously unbalanced. For example, the most influential and generally acceptable book on the healing ministry published in Great Britain this century is probably Weatherhead's *Psychology, Religion and Healing*, which, whilst published only in 1951, is quite insensitive in this matter. A legitimate and valuable discussion of the possible aetiology, therapy, and results of the healings is quite unbalanced by any serious consideration of what these events probably meant to the early Church. The result is that sometimes in this discussion Christ seems to have been only a great psychiatrist, born out of due season and owing his pre-eminence to the unequalled rapidity and completeness of his cures. A most precarious position in these days of pharmaco-logical wonders!

The principal Greek words used to describe 'to cure', 'to heal', 'to make whole', etc.; are given in the table that follows:

Greek Word	Usual A.V. Translation	All O.T. Usages	Uses in a clinical context						Uses outside a clinical context	
			All Gospels	Matthew	Mark	Luke	John	Elsewhere in N.T.	Gospels	Elsewhere in N.T.
θεραπεύειν	heal		35	13	8	13	1	5	0	0
ἰάομαι	heal		17	3	1	11	2	4	2	2
σώζειν	made whole	350	13	3	5	5	0	2	38	48
καθαρίζειν	cleanse		12	4	3	5	0	0	4	14
ἀποκαθίστημι	restore whole		4	1	2	1	0	0	2	2

To cleanse (καθαρίζειν)

This word differs from the others in having not only a clear theological distinction, but also a clear medical one. This is because certain diseases of the skin were traditionally for Juda-ism amongst those conditions which rendered a man unclean and debarred him from priesthood and Inner Temple. The healing of lepers is therefore a natural symbol of the end of the Old Covenant and the giving of a new one.

Where this word is used in a medical context it is always a leper who is cured, e.g. Matt. 8:2; 10:8; 11:5; Mk. 1:41; Lk. 17:14. As is well known, it is improbable that the skin disease from which these men suffered was leprosy. For our purpose it is sufficient to note that it was a disease of the skin which rendered a man ceremonially unclean, and did the same to anyone who came into contact with him. Ceremonial uncleanness was the great fear of the devout Jew, for it excluded him from religious observances, and so from the possibility of salvation. We find the same word (καθαρίζειν) used in non-medical contexts in Matt. 23:25; 27:59; Jn. 2:6.[1]

'To cleanse' (καθαρίζειν) is used of the removal of those medical conditions which seem to portray the rottenness and sinfulness of man's life, the part which is most abhorrent to mankind.[2] There is a sense of disgust, and the use of 'uncleanness' to describe it, the fear of spread by touch, and the use of ceremonial washing to remove it are all congruous. For this reason the cleansing of the lepers by Christ is relevant both to the immediate dissolving of the Old Israel by the establishment of the New Israel (the Jewish Christ) and to the salvation of everyman from the corruption of the flesh in which he feels himself incarcerated (the Man Christ). Christ by healing the lepers attacks the Pharasaic representatives of the Old Israel (Matt. 23:25), and we are reminded that this incarnate work is connected with Peter's vision at Joppa—'What God has cleansed [ἐκαθάρισεν] that call not thou common' (Acts 10:15). There is a result wider than Judaism, however, for when Christ touches the leper, he unites the leper's flesh to his flesh, for he was made flesh (σάρξ ἐγεννητός) and even that part of human nature has in his Incarnation been taken up into the Godhead. The cleansing of the lepers is part of the sacrificial redemptive act, not excluded from it as in Judaism.[3] Such an act means that Christ can be present doing his saving work when the Church offers acceptable sacrifices to God through its nurses and home-helps as they perform intimate and unpleasant ablutionary acts

[1] This miracle at Cana in Galilee of changing the Judaistic water of purifying into the wine of the New Covenant (Baptismal water and Holy Communion wine) seems for St John to replace the healing of a leper in the Synoptics, of which there is no mention in John's Gospel.

[2] Psychiatry teaches us how often a deep sense of guilt and disgust may be exteriorised in a lesion about the 'bad' part, producing a rash on say the hand or about the genital region. In obsessional states there may be unending washings of the hands, or terrible concern about toilet matters.

[3] It is not meant to be implied that Judaism did not encourage or practise good works. Far from it. But these works were separated off by cultic practices from the inner sanctuary of the Temple. Fear of uncleanness was a practical obstruction to works of mercy.

for the sick person. What a contrast to the Judaism of Christ's time, when following such an act complicated ritual cleansing was necessary before the person could offer sacrifice.

We may be sure that the stories of Christ's cleansing of the lepers played a prominent part in instruction for Baptism and disputes with Judaism. The story of Naaman the leper (Lk. 4:27 and 2 Kings 4:14) must also have been important in the mission to the Gentile.

'To heal', translating θεραπεύειν and ἰάομαι

These two Greek words are dealt with together, because there seems no certain theological or medical distinction between them. It has been suggested that, without prejudice to the result, θεραπεύειν means to treat, in the technical medical sense of looking after a patient.[1] ἰάομαι then means to achieve the desired result, a 'cure' as we say. Whilst there are passages in the New Testament in which this would make sense, there are others where it is most improbable. Most of the usages of ἰάομαι come from Luke, as the above table shows, and perhaps they are all derived from him originally. There is an interesting point here for textual scholars. Unless they can give us additional information, we have only the general impression that these two words are generally interchangeable, with a possible reservation that ἰάομαι is sometimes more positive, announcing the successful result which was expected when the disciples acted, and certain when Jesus' work was not obstructed by unfaith. If there is such a distinction, then it is smaller than that between these two words and the others. For these two words are distinguished by having no particular Judaistic associations of the kind which καθαρίζειν, σώζειν and ἀποκαθίστημι possess. They are also distinguished from καθαρίζειν and σώζειν, but similar to ἀποκαθίστημι in being predominantly used in the narrative indirect speech, and hardly ever in the direct speech of Jesus. σώζειν is nearly always found in the direct speech of Jesus to the one he heals, καθαρίζειν frequently, but θεραπεύειν and ἰάομαι never.

Examples of θεραπεύειν are to be found in Matt. 4:23; 8:7; 17:18; Mk. 1:34; 3:2; Lk. 5:15; 9:6; Jn. 5:10.

[1] Weatherhead, op. cit., p. 79, n. 9.

The word is used predominantly in the narrative, and partly in the direct speech of Jesus in the Sabbath day controversies and in the commissioning of the Twelve and Seventy, but *never* by Jesus speaking to the healed person.

There are examples of ἰάομαι in Matt. 8:8; 15:28; Mk. 5:29; Lk. 5:17; 6:19; 8:47; 17:15.

We note here that there is no use of ἰάομαι to report the speech of Jesus. Every use is in the narrative.

ἀποκαθίστημι, translated 'restore whole', is used eight times in the New Testament. One use, in Heb. 13:19 seems to have neither medical nor theological significance. It is used three times of the man with the withered hand (Matt. 12:13; Mk. 3:5; Lk. 6:10), once of Blind Bartimeus (Mk. 10:46–52), and three times of the restoration of Israel (Mk. 8:25; Matt. 17:11; Acts 1:6). It seems possible that the Evangelists deliberately used this word to describe the healing of the man with the withered hand and Blind Bartimeus, to suggest that Jesus was the New Elijah come to restore Israel.

Before turning to our main study of σώζειν we must mention a number of words used only once:

ἀπολέλυσαι (Lk. 13:12) 'Woman thou art *loosed* from thine infirmities.' We are reminded of the bondage of sin and the Pauline idea of a ransom for a slave.
ἀνορθόω (Lk. 13:13) 'immediately she was *made straight*'.
The only other use is in Acts 15:16, quoting Amos 9:11 referring to the restoration of David's tabernacle.
ὑγιαίνοντα (Lk. 7:10) 'found the servant *whole*'.
ἐπέστρεψεν (Lk. 8:55) 'her spirit *came again*'.

σέσωκέν, usually translated 'saved' in a theological context and 'made whole' in a medical context, is used one hundred and two times in the New Testament.

Context	Gospels	Mt.	Mk.	Lk.	Jn.	Act.	Rom.	1 Cor.	Tim.	Ja.	Pt.	Others	Total
Medical	13	3	5	5	0	2	0	0	0	0	0	0	(15)
Theological	25	7	7	6	5	9	6	8	6	5	2	12	(73)
Other	12	5	2	4	1	2	0	0	0	0	0	0	(14)

To deal with the 'other' uses first. Whilst not theological in the sense of the seventy-three instances they may have theological implications just as when the word is used in a medical context. They are concerned either with saving from or in water, or with the passion. Examples of the first are Matt. 8:25; 14:30; Acts 27:31. It is possible that these accounts may have been used with a baptismal reference, as well as to comfort those who felt themselves sinking under the burden of sin. It is the same Peter who says 'Lord, save us; we perish' who says 'baptism does also now save [σώζει] us' (1 Pet. 3:21). We must also remember that Baptism may sometimes have been by total immersion, so that there was a real sinking into the waves to rise again saved by the Lord Jesus. On these occasions, words like Peter's may have been uttered. Examples of the word being used of the Passion are Matt. 27:40; Mk. 15:31; Jn. 12:27.

There are seventy-three uses of σώζειν in a strict theological sense. In this sense it means salvation from the bondage of sin, sickness, meaninglessness, death, and judgment. It also means salvation into freedom from the bondage of sin, into health and life eternal now and hereafter. It means entry into a new man and a new age and a new life hid with God in Christ. These are some examples: Matt. 1:21; 24:13; Mk. 16:16; 13:20; Lk. 8:12; 13:23; Jn. 3:17; 12:27; Acts 2:21; 2:47; 11:14; 16:30f; Rom. 5:10; 11:26; 1 Cor. 3:15; 9:22; 1 Tim. 1:15; Jam. 2:14; 1 Pet. 3:21. A fact which this selection does not reveal is the number of occasions where salvation has an obvious eschatological reference. It is being saved in the Day of the Lord that is in mind (e.g. Matt. 24:13; 24:22; Mk. 13:13, 20; Lk. 9:24; Jn. 12:47). Because Jesus' healing works are signs of the times the use of σώζειν is most suitable.

We are here at the very centre of the Christian Gospel, for it is the announcement of this salvation which is the climax of the apostolic preaching. It was to illustrate what this salvation meant, to authorise their teaching, and to declare one way in which it had already come, that the records of Christ's healing works were cherished by the early Church, not as standards of health or psychosomatic normality, but as signs of the Great Deliverance. This is not to deny that they may have valuable lessons for us today about health and psychosomatic normality.

The common use of σώζειν for salvation from sin and from disease reaffirms the Hebraic view of the close relation between sin and suffering and between healing and salvation. It is used fifteen times in a medical context in the New Testament, twelve times in the Gospels, and twice in Acts. In ten cases the A.V. translates this as 'made whole', in four cases 'healed', and once 'saved'.

Matt. 9:21. 'If I may but touch his garment I *shall be whole.*' (*A*) (σωθήσομαι)

Matt. 9:22. 'He [Jesus] said, Thy faith has made thee *whole.*' (*A*) (σέσωκέν)

Matt. 9:22. 'And the woman was *made whole* from that hour.' (*A*) (ἐσώθη)

Mk. 5:23 'Lay thy hands upon her that she may *be healed.*' (*B*) (σωθῇ)

Mk. 5:28. 'If I may but touch his clothes I shall *be whole.*' (*A*) (σωθήσομαι)

Mk. 5:34. 'He [Jesus] said unto her, Daughter, thy faith hath made thee *whole.*' (*A*) (σέσωκέν)

Mk. 6:56. 'As many as touched him were *made whole.*' (*C*) (ἐσώζοντα)

Lk. 8:36. 'He that was possessed of the devil was *healed.*' (ἐσώθη)

Lk. 8:48. 'He [Jesus] said . . . thy faith has made thee *whole*; go in peace.' (*A*) (σέσωκέν)

Lk. 8:50. 'He [Jesus] said . . . believe only, and she shall be *made whole.*' (*D*) (σωθήσεται)

Lk. 17:19. 'He [Jesus] said Arise go thy way thy faith has made thee whole.' (*D*) (σέσωκέν)

Lk. 18:42. 'Jesus said, Receive thy sight: thy faith hath *made thee whole.*' (*C*) (σέσωκέν)

Acts 4:9. 'the impotent man, by what means he was *made whole.*' (σέσωσται)

Acts 14:9. 'he had faith to be *healed.*' (σωθῆναι)

We may also mention here a non-medical story, the forgiveness of the woman who was a sinner (Lk. 7:50).

Lk. 7:50. 'He [Jesus] said . . . thy faith hath *saved* thee: go in peace.' (σέσωκέν)

(*A*) Indicates the woman with the issue of blood.

(*B*) Indicates the ruler of the Synagogue's daughter.

(*C*) Indicates Blind Bartimeus.

(*D*) Indicates the tenth leper.

What are the general impressions which these usages of σώζειν in a medical context give us?

1. They are largely not in narrative but spoken words.

2. A large proportion are words of Jesus spoken directly to the person he has healed.

3. The Evangelists have gone out of their way to use σώζειν and not θεραπεύειν or ἰάομαι in Jesus' direct words to the healed.

4. They are of the pattern:

    (*a*) A coming to Jesus.

    (*b*) A calling of his Name.

    (*c*) Faith in his Name.

    (*d*) A touch.

    (*e*) 'Made whole' or 'saved' (and 'cleansed' if we remember the direct words of Jesus to the lepers).

    (*f*) Go in peace.

    (*g*) Rejoicing.

Are we very close here to words and acts used by Jesus and subsequently by his disciples and the earliest Church, when men and women came to be received and/or blessed in acts of blessing, of Baptism or of healing? In this connection we recall the very early speeches of Peter in Acts chs. 2, 3, 4 where the healing of the lame man at the Gate Beautiful is 'mixed up with' the preaching of the Gospel, the calling for repentance and Baptism into a New Life. It is here that we find one of the two medical usages of σώζειν in Acts (4:9; 14:9). It is the same Peter who speaks in Acts 4 who says later in his letter 'baptism does now save us' (σώζει) (1 Pet. 3:21).

It seems possible that the use of σώζειν in the healing miracles, whether translated in the A.V. by 'healed', 'saved', or 'made whole', was largely dictated by the needs of the early Church to teach a theological lesson, probably about Baptism, and to supply suitable liturgical material for use at baptisms. There is a lot of movement in the passages concerned: a coming to Jesus, a calling upon his name, a desire to be touched, a touching, a being made whole and a receiving of sight, and a movement outwards—a going in peace and a leaping and rejoicing and giving thanks.

If we can imagine a baptismal scene when ecstasy was still prevalent, as we know it was in the early Church from Pauline references to 'speaking with tongues', then the possibility of a free atmosphere presents itself. We can imagine men and women actually calling on the name of Jesus as they plunged into the waters, and calling out that they were cleansed and saved as they came from the waters. We can imagine these being told to go in peace, but leaping and dancing and glorifying God and following the Way. No doubt it soon became necessary to enforce new order, to give formal instruction to those wishing for Baptism, and produce a more sober liturgy.

Even then phrases like 'Thy faith has made thee whole' (ἡ πίστις σου σέσωκέν σε) or 'Go in peace' may have been regularly used.

The medical σώζειν passages are designed to show the need of, requirements for, and effects of Baptism. They are not designed to show either the medical effects of faith or to show the medical qualities of standard full health, and whilst we may legitimately use them for that purpose we must take care not to press them too far in a usage for which they were never primarily intended. We may legitimately use them because of the traditional Judaistic relationship between sin and disease, and because the healing works of Jesus which are used as illustrations were in fact real works, not just weak symbols but effective signs.

'Thy faith hath saved thee'

This phrase, used several times by Christ after healing the sick, and used after the forgiveness of a woman who was a sinner, quite rightly commends itself to those who are eager to forward the Church's ministry of healing. The prominent part given by the evangelists (and therefore presumably by the very early Church) to the healing work of Jesus, together with the employment of the phrase 'Thy faith hath saved thee', shows that they regarded these as most illuminating examples of what Christ had done and would continue to do for men. He would lift them by the hand. He would open their eyes which could not see him, and their ears which could not hear him, and the tongue which could not praise him. The recurrence of the phrase is very striking, and suggests the possibility that these are the very words used by Christ, and perhaps preserved by liturgical usage. They would be very appropriate immediately after Baptism. They demonstrate again the close connection in the mind of the Jews of Christ's time between the burden of sin and the burden of disease. By the common usage of 'saved' for what faith in Christ does for the sick man and for the sinner the states of sin and redemption, sickness and healing, are made to illuminate each other. So a 'healthy' man is one who has been saved by faith in Christ; he has been joined to him in a life of obedience to the Father, love of all men, self-sacrifice and suffering, joy and crucifixion. Conversely a 'redeemed' man is one who shares in Christ's reversal of the work of Adam, whose flesh shares in the making of all things new, the cosmological redemption, and so can share physically and materially in what Christ has done for mankind, whether through anti-slavery legislation or antibiotic research or the mercy of a home-help. The mutual illumination of 'healing' and 'redemption', 'wholeness' and 'salvation' rests on historic fact, the fact that there was in Palestine under Christ, and there is in the world under Christ today, a real relation between health and redemption. But both our spiritual state and our physical health share in the consequences that follow from the fact that we live in the times between Christ's having struck the decisive blow, and the final rounding up of all the forces of evil. We continue to sin after Baptism, and perfect faith and perfect Christian life is claimed by no Christian. We continue after baptism to inhabit bodies and minds which are part of a fallen world, and so perfect health is known by no Christian. If perfection of either health or sinlessness is claimed, it is no part of the apostolic tradition, for St Paul gloried neither in being free from sin (cf. 1 Tim. 1:15; Eph. 3:8; 1 Cor. 15:9) or free from infirmity (cf. 11 Cor. 12). Quite apart from our own personal imperfections, so that 'if we say that we have no sin, we deceive ourselves, and the truth is not in us' (1 Jn. 1:8), we do not escape by our faith from our communion with other men and with nature. For, as we have stressed, the natural involvement of men one with another and with the whole cosmos, means that the sin and sickness of one affects all, and the sin and sickness of all affects the one. Therefore although there is a very real and observable connection between faith and physical healing, as there is between faith and the burden of sin, it is neither a total connection nor a mathematical ratio. Our communion with nature and other men means that we share their predicament. So long as there are earthquakes and mankind suffers them, no man is exempt from that suffering. So long as there is a man with a cosh in his hand mankind must suffer this man's sin, and no man is exempt from that suffering. So long as there is one man with the genetic formation which transmits diabetes mellitus, mankind must suffer this and no man is exempt from that suffering. Now the 'faith' (πίστις) which Jesus commends is, as we have already asserted, acceptance of Jesus Christ as Saviour. It is an identification of man with Christ, a committal of the whole person to be in Christ and Christ in him, analogous to the way in which a man and woman commit themselves to each other in marriage to be one flesh: 'For better, for worse, for richer, for poorer, in sickness and in health.' To have faith is to assent to what Christ has already done when he joined himself to all men. The result of faith is not merely to be joined to Christ, and dying with him to be raised with him, thus to enjoy release from the power of sin and sickness, but also at the very same moment, to be joined with Christ to the whole sinful, sick world, and thus bear with Christ a heavy burden. To use a crude analogy, we at one and the same time fit an infinitely powerful engine and take on an infinite load of sick and sinful passengers, and to use a concrete example, we perhaps are freed from rheumatoid arthritis and go to the mission field to share with Christ our brothers' malarial parasites and anti-malarial drugs. Or perhaps we are freed from fornication and go to the field of local politics and share with others who are working there the sinful but inescapable compromises which are involved.

Faith in Jesus, and coming to him to be touched, are therefore the means of being saved and of being made whole, and if we wish to know some of the qualities of wholeness of life for usage in medico-sociological work we may study the qualities

of the 'saved life' as portrayed in the New Testament. Legitimately we may ask those who are studying the 'saved life' of
Christians to study the insights given by modern medical,
psychological, and sociological insights, but the Christian must
not suffer from a failure of theological nerve. He must ask
himself what the New Testament says about the life of health
and then see that he and others in their researches and pronouncements do not overlook these aspects. This is not to
replace scientific observation by Scripture, but to insist that
science address itself to some of the problems which Christians
believe may well be crucial human problems.

We must now ask what the New Testament says about the
saved, healed, or whole life to which the phrase 'Thy faith hath
made thee whole' refers. We may then bear this in mind in our
discussions with medicine, sociology, and philosophy. To do
this theme justice would require a whole book or library of
books; we must therefore confine ourselves to the communal
aspects of the saved, whole life. We can say that the definition
for Christians of a 'whole man' is epitomised in the 'whole' life
of Christ, his disciples, and the early Church, a life of fellowship
with man, of loving the weak, of power and praise and prayer,
of full living and full suffering, of preaching and healing.

If we consider first the use of σώζειν in the Old Testament,
we may fairly say that there is a considerable emphasis upon
its corporate aspects. This is of course balanced in some places
in Ezekiel, in the Wisdom literature, and in the Psalms, where
a majority of some seventy-five uses of σώζειν are personal, but
the corporate aspect is strong and teaches us that 'to be saved'
or 'to be made whole' is to enjoy a deliverance from defeat and
destruction together with others. At first this salvation concerns
itself largely with the immediate battles against enemies of
Israel and with memories of past deliverances of God's people,
but later there is emphasis on the future deliverance of the
righteous remnant of Israel or the righteous of all nations on
the day of the Lord. On 'that day' whosoever shall call on the
name of the Lord shall be saved. To be 'made whole' in the Old
Testament is to be made one with all those who are saved. We
must remember that in so far as the Jews of Christ's time believed in a resurrection it was largely a corporate and corporal

8

resurrection in which all the righteous were raised simultaneously. The Greek view of the 'good', central part of man, his 'soul', continuing to live after death by virtue of its essentially immortal property, held little interest for the Hebrew mind compared with the conception of a mighty act of God whereby on the Day of his Judgment he would raise all the righteous and bring the whole material universe directly under his rule. This corporate and often eschatological usage of σώζειν continues in the New Testament. These are some examples from the thirty-eight usages in the Gospels, excluding the other thirteen usages which are in a medical context: (Matt. 1:21; 10:22; 24:22; Lk. 13:23; Jn. 12:47). Examples from the forty-eight uses of σώζειν in the rest of the New Testament are to be found in Acts 2:21; Rom. 5:9; 9:27; 11 Thess. 2:10; Jude 5; Rev. 21:24.

As has been said in a previous chapter, the corporate aspects of God's work are less overt in the New Testament than in the Old. Whilst in the writings of St Paul there are few direct statements that salvation is corporate, the many 'models' of salvation which he uses are corporate. Thus, for example, for St Paul baptism was a dying with Christ and a rising again with him out of the waters to a state of salvation or wholeness. This may sound very individualistic, but when we remember that St Paul sees baptism as Christian circumcision (Rom. 4:1), and that circumcision is a sign of being grafted into membership with Israel, the people of God, we realise that to 'be made whole' is to be joined to a group chosen to accomplish a particular task of God. St Paul also portrays baptism, the entry into salvation, the 'making whole', in terms of the model of the crossing of the Red Sea, with Christ as the new Moses (1 Cor. 10:1–5). To be made whole, therefore, is to join others who have with Christ crossed the Red Sea and must fight and suffer with their leader to enter the Promised Land. Also St Paul writes that to be baptised, to be 'saved' is to be made one with many, 'for in one Spirit were we all baptised into one body, whether Jews or Greeks, whether bond or free; and were all made to drink of one Spirit'[1] (1 Cor. 12:13). For St Paul, baptism, when men and women, like the woman with an issue of blood, or like

---

[1] Drinking reminds us that in some primitive baptisms the water was drunk and also that Christ was present with a 'cup of cold water only'.

Blind Bartimeus are saved, or 'made whole' by faith in Christ, is an occasion not only of personal deliverance but of being joined, made one, made whole with Christ and with those others to whom Christ has joined himself (cf. 1 Cor. 12:13–17).[1] Not least amongst those to whom Christ has joined himself are the sick, the weak, and the suffering. To be 'saved', 'healed', or 'made whole' by faith in Christ is to enter a community of suffering, and to have new experience of suffering and the Resurrection triumph of Christ. This is the wholeness of the 'Communion of Saints'.

We may now consider the prevalent view of health and whether the corporate aspects of the biblical concept of wholeness has anything to say about it. The prevalent view of health is no longer that of optimum local efficiencies, all aggregated to give a satisfactory total of achievement, but rather of harmony between the different bodily systems of the individual and between the individual organism and his environment. There is a strong return to the Greek concept of the 'mean' and of *harmonia*. Allied to this is a general and usually unrecognised assumption that the individual would achieve this harmony but for the fact that unfortunate experiences condition him to something less than 'wholeness'. These unfortunate experiences range in different schools from accidents in childhood leading to deformities of the skeleton, to deprivation of love in infancy leading to deformities of the mind. In such thought it is often optimistically presupposed that given adequate environmental conditions the individual will achieve a wholeness of body and mind, which will be recognised subjectively by a sense of well-being and objectively by making relationships with other people which society recognises as satisfactory. Conversely, if the individual is internally harmonised, and has a sense of well-being, and has satisfactory relationships with others, then the child born to her will develop satisfactorily. There is new recognition of the diversity of faculties which human beings possess, and which must grow in harmony with each other and with the similar faculties of others, and the new medical humanists give much place and sometimes pride of place to

---

[1] Cf. Flemington, W. F., *The New Testament Doctrine of Baptism* (S.P.C.K., 1948) where these aspects of St Paul's thought are dealt with fully.

'spiritual' factors and the need to love and be loved. Into materialistic medicine, with its compartmentalism, have come some corporate models in which balance and harmony and interactionism play the major part, and of late religion has been added for good measure, but the same assumption of evolutionary progress is made: namely, that if only adverse conditions can be removed a person will achieve 'wholeness'. The circularity of the definitions of the goals is also often overlooked by using as norms scientific terms which are not realised to be value judgments. The commonest among psychiatrists is 'reality testing', and the 'whole' person is one who does not deceive himself about reality, as for instance, when by gross racial prejudice—say by unjustifiable and scientifically insupportable beliefs about negroes—one escapes from the painful necessity of treating them as equals. However, whilst this test may be relatively satisfactory when the nature of some simple phenomenon is in question, it becomes useless when one is concerned with the question at the level we are discussing it —i.e., what is full health; for the question as to what life 'really' is (and thus a standard for reality testing) ceases to be a scientific one as soon as one leaves the laboratory.

The trouble, from the biblical point of view, is that whilst the modern view of wholeness often has much in common with that large part of Christian teaching which sees man's struggle as one for goals of perfection, salvation, or sanctification, it disregards at least three other important aspects of the biblical doctrine of man. First, that the satisfactory community relations required of man extend beyond this universe and beyond this life. The community with whose health the Bible is concerned is not bounded by the grave, it is the Communion of Saints. The goal set for man is that he shall love both God and his neighbour as himself. Second, that in terms of human striving for perfection Christ is the pattern of that perfection. Third, that the power, the means of achieving such communion are provided by God. The power to love God and neighbour is given by God and received by a personal act of faith which is above reason, yet not outside it, and Christ who is the object of that faith is also the 'express image' of the love which is the substance and goal of the one made 'whole'. The trouble with the modern concept of health, even when it receives a full middle-class treatment,[1] is that it tells people to be what they are—'good chaps'. At its highest it tells men and women to find their life by losing it in acts of love-faith, but to questions as to the definition of 'love-faith' it can only answer that it is a kind of living which personal experience or psychiatric opinion finds to result in being the kind of person you or the psychiatrist or society feels that you are—or should be. 'Faith' and 'love' are what personal and social experience of the time sees them to be. The Christian teaching is that God is love and that Christ is the express image of God, and therefore if the Christian takes this seriously there is in the whole life and words of Christ an image of love, of health, and of 'wholeness'. This is not to dispense with the medical and social arts but to ask biblical questions of them, and bring their answers to the Bible to illuminate them. When, for example, as now, one hears some Christian psychiatrists assert that a 'whole life', a Christian life, is a life of loving and that the type of true loving is that of the psychotherapeutic interview in which the psychiatrist never expresses value judgments or labels any action as culpable, as sin, we may ask ourselves whether this is the love of Christ. We shall not easily allow such extravagant statements, even when supported by chosen texts from the New Testament, if they run clean contrary to an essential element in Christ's life. If God is Love, and Christ is the express image of God, then the life of love which we must live, the saved life into which we enter when we are 'made whole', will be like his. It will issue first from the Father and respond to the Father's love, for 'herein is love, not that we loved God, but that he loved us' (1 Jn. 4:10). The loving will include suffering, receiving sinners with understanding, urging others to repent, relieving distress, prophesying, and expression of anger. It is not only 'gentle Jesus' who loves, but also the law-giver Jesus, the prophet Jesus, the judge Jesus who loves, and the objective of love is that Christ may be made present to all, that through him by faith all present may be saved, 'made whole'. Here we must remember the corporate aspect of σώζειν. The salvation or

---

[1] Cf. Chamberlain, V. C., *Adolescence to Maturity*: A practical guide to personal development, fulfilment and maturity. An excellent Penguin handbook for the adolescent.

wholeness which is received through response of faith to love is the admittance to the people of God, into a unity of people who are called to be the means under God of the salvation, the making whole, of all peoples. To be made whole is to be part of the corporate suffering servant by whose stripes others, and ultimately all men, will be healed. This is why, until the last days, when this task is completed, to receive the words 'Thy faith hath made thee whole' is to enter into a fellowship which, like its Master's not only has power over evil and sin, manifested in graceful and true lives, but also is joined to sin; and as it joins itself to sin, and heals sin, it suffers. Like its Master, the suffering servant, the people of God suffer in mind, body, and spirit as a unity. We must beware of those who agree with the fact that Christian wholeness involves suffering, but suppose that the man made whole by faith will only suffer on a 'higher' plane, so that he is relieved of his duodenal ulcer but is visited by mental suffering. This is equivalent to the saying that the Incarnation of God in Christ did not involve true suffering in the flesh. Such people would omit the Cross and place the Ascension immediately after the Agony in Gethsemene. It may well be that the salvation by faith into the people of God may mean the healing of a man's duodenal ulcer which was caused by worries which are now felt to be only trivialities; but on the other hand the fit and healthy young man without a worry in the world may be by faith 'made whole' into a change of job which will put him at risk to all sorts of new physical, mental, and moral dangers. We are reminded of those people who during the last war by change of circumstance experienced change of health: the man who left behind his peptic ulcer and his wife for active service but lost an arm through shrapnel, or the man who found a fellowship and a purpose in war service which showed his previous life to be but a half-life, but whose mind ultimately broke under the load it carried.

Is there then no real change on balance when a man is 'made whole'? The answer here is, as we would expect, the answer to the same question when asked of baptism. A man becomes what he potentially is, one with Christ, and thereby one with man and God. The result is that he shares in the fellowship of those who experience now a taste (ἀρραβών) of the powers of the

age to come. It is this taste of the power of God, this work of
the Holy Spirit, which we experience in ourselves and witness in
others. These visible fruits of the Spirit are seen as turning from
sin, and as diverse gifts of which the greatest is an outpouring
of love for God and men. Such real changes in the psyche
inevitably mean real changes in the soma which sometimes may
be 'minute', as in the change in the facial muscles producing a
smile, and sometimes may be 'large', as the reversal of the
progress of asthmatic disease, rheumatoid arthritis, hyper-
tension, or peptic ulcer. These changes are such as one would
predict if one had perfect knowledge of the pathology of human
disease, which no one has and never will have. They are not a
measure of the 'wholeness' or spiritual changes of the person
concerned, if we consider wholeness as a condition of union of
the whole person with the Whole Christ. The measure of
whether the sick man is made whole will be whether in him and
through him the sacrament of the making present of the Saviour
is performed. The sickness of the patient is not merely a negative thing, of which no positive good can come, and of which the
most that can be expected is its removal. It is the very means
chosen by God to save the patient and the community around
him. Men and women are, in the words of St John, sick 'that
the works of God should be made manifest in [him] them'.
The 'works of God' here mentioned are of course the salvation
of mankind, and this means that through the sick man, Christ
in his earthly Ministry, and now Christ in his Church, brings
men and women into the taste of the saved community life, the
eternal life community. Thus, as we were at pains to show
earlier, the Gospel healings were occasions of community
judgment when many entered into eternal life in the saved
community, and many rejected it. The sickness of the community, present in one of their members, is there 'that the
works of God should be made manifest in them', that is, that
the community through their obedience permit Christ to remember in them what he did with sickness and suffering in his
earthly ministry. Together with Christ the High Priest on
High, the sick man and the Church around him offer their
sickness and healing compassion and receive grace. The sick
person concerned may be in a terminal illness, and his death

may be prolonged or expedited according to the operation of imperfectly understood mechanisms, but through him many may be saved. This, indeed, is the sadness of the failure of men and women to offer their sickness and compassion to God in Christ, for not only is the recovery rate depressed, though this is vitally important, but the occasion of salvation has been neglected. When men and women, seeing the sick man in their midst, offer their lives in service to the sick man they offer their lives to Christ. They are joined to Christ in his Mystical Body, and they enter with him into salvation; the sick man is joined to them, and together they enter with Christ into the new wholeness. Even if we are primarily concerned with physical cures, this means that these are to be looked for not only in the sick man but also in the community. So a man who has a congenital defect, about which he is chronically embittered, may be saved by the loving service and prayers of another person or group, and yet retain his congenital deformity, whilst one of the group who has been involved may be relieved of a peptic ulcer. This type of situation is exemplified by the dying patient who makes of dying, as of life, not just 'one damn thing after another', but a 'reasonable, lively, and holy sacrifice', a time of growing in wisdom and stature. Those who are near to him, and serving him, and easing his pain, enter, if they wish, into the wholeness into which he by faith has entered, and altogether with Christ are made perfect in suffering. So the community in acts of healing, relieving suffering, and suffering together, enters the Communion of Saints, that is, the community of those made whole. This community extends beyond this universe and extends beyond the grave. It is the fellowship (*koinonia*) of the Body of Christ, and is both the product and the means of loving one another and having all things, including sickness, common. The Church's ministry of healing is, like all its ministry, a declaring and a doing of what it is, the saving Body of Christ. In the doing of the ministry of healing, those concerned in it become little Christs, and this is why we shall suggest later that the sick man and those who love him and strive to heal him might well be anointed together, as an effective sign that they are made Christs who are sent to save others. Is this not what chrism means? Or alternatively, as we shall also suggest, the taking of Holy Communion to the sick must mean the taking of Christ in the local church visibly to surround the sick man's bed and have communion with him. Thus, quite literally, the sickness of a man or woman becomes the occasion when the Church joins with him to receive Christ in its midst, and the Church goes on its way rejoicing and saying 'Thy [our] faith hath made us [thee] whole.'

CHAPTER 9

THE LOCAL CHURCH, THE
LITURGICAL MOVEMENT, AND
THE HEALTH OF THE LOCAL
COMMUNITY

THERE IS THROUGHOUT the world today, in every
Christian denomination, a movement to break down the
artificial barriers between work and worship, between minister
and layman, between the church building and the Church,
between churchgoers in the parish and all men and women in
the parish area. The corporate concepts which we have expounded are taken seriously, and the local church is regarded as
being called to be what it is, the people of God and the body of
Christ. As such they are to be one, not only with one another in
a cultic church group, but also with the whole neighbourhood.
They are, in acts of love, to be what they already are by their
baptism with Christ, brothers of all men, and especially of those
who carry heavy burdens. This movement has come to be
known as the Liturgical Movement, a name which is liable to
be seriously misunderstood by those who think of liturgy as
complicated, ecclesiastically-centred procedures of a 'High
Church' kind. This is not the intention of the movement, for
which 'liturgy' means rather the whole action and work of the
Body of Christ, the people of God, the local church fellowship,
when it offers, in Christ, its whole life as a sacrifice to God.
This offering of itself is done in the offering of Christ, and means
a continual going out of Christians from worship within the
church building to continue worship in acts of love in the local
scene. With a strong corporate and sociological emphasis, much
is made of the necessity of a planned community approach, and
of team-work in its accomplishment.[1]

[1] A useful précis of the Liturgical Movement, together with a bibliography, is
given by Shands, A. R., in *The Liturgical Movement and the Local Church*, S.C.M.
Press, 1959.

From the realisation that the Christian life is sharing in a common life, sharing in the one loaf, sharing in the one Spirit, there has been a rediscovery that fellowship is the nature, the mark, the fruit, and the condition of Christian life. Realising, too, that the present structure of society is such that the root family group is constantly being broken up by the growing freedom and mobility of Man, and that the modern ethos tends to aggravate the perennial temptation to separate work from worship, the Liturgical Movement has deliberately looked to the small group level at which these divisions can not only best be healed but seen to be healed. So we have the 'house-church', in which the Christian group, gathered from within the immediate neighbourhood of the adjacent houses, centres its liturgy. A liturgy expressed in offerings which range from scrubbing out a kitchen, or celebrating the Holy Communion from the kitchen table, to local political action about the provision of indoor water-closets in houses in the same street. Each man and woman offers this liturgy as a member of his house-church, which itself does so as the representative of the Church-in-the-parish.

In this work of being the Body within the parish, the parish church must concern itself with all men and with the whole lives of all men. Particularly, like Christ, they must identify themselves with those who suffer, whether in mind, body, or estate. Of the burdens which men and women carry, the burdens of disease are amongst the greatest, and if the Church is to be what it is, then it must speak and act to this situation. We shall now consider how the parish church may be obedient to its Head in this matter.

The visitation of the sick

Because the visitation of the sick is a traditional way in which the Church has set about continuing Christ's good works, and because many Christians today feel that what is already being done in this direction fully covers the Church's ministry to the sick, it is worth starting from the 'visitation' in our consideration of the theology of the local church's liturgy to the sick in the parish. By starting from 'visiting' we start from something already known and practised.

'Pure religion and undefiled before God and the Father is this, to visit [ἐπισκέπτεσθαι] the fatherless and widows in their affliction' (Jam. 1:27).

'I was sick, and ye visited [ἐπεσκέψασθέ] me' (Matt. 25:36).

'Feed the flock of God which is amongst you, taking the oversight [ἐπισκοποῦντες] thereof, not by constraint, but willingly' (1 Pet. 5:2).

'Because thou knewest not the time of thy visitation [ἐπισκοπῆς]' (Lk. 19:44—cf. 1 Pet. 2:12).

'Blessed be the Lord God of Israel; for he hath visited [ἐπεσκέψατο] and redeemed his people' (Lk. 1:68).

'Whereby the dayspring from on high hath visited [ἐπισκέψεται] us' (Lk. 1:78).

'For a bishop [ἐπίσκοποι] must be blameless . . .' (Titus 1:7).

'Ecclesiastical visitations, originally the periodical journeys of personal inspections to ascertain the temporal and spiritual condition of each parish, form part of the functions of an arch-bishop, bishop, or archdeacon.' (*Enc. Britt.*)

It comes as a surprise to find that the word 'visit', which we associate with visiting the sick, is a translation of a word which has as its cognates '*episketomai*', which is close to '*episkipio*', from which our 'bishop' is derived, and is close to the use of the word when we say that God 'visits' and redeems his people. A 'visit' is also, we see above, a day of judgment for Jerusalem; and when the bishop 'visits' a parish he concerns himself with the temporal and spiritual welfare of his people. Evidently the visitation of the sick is not only taking old Mrs Jones a home-made cake, though it certainly is that, but something more like what God does when he comes to his people. It is something like the bishop coming to his flock. Conversely, the *episkopos* (bishop) appointed by the whole Christ, acts as one appointed and sent by the whole Christ to be a 'church visitor'. In him Christ-in-the-Church visits and redeems his people. So when the layman 'visits' the sick he goes like the bishop, that is, he goes as representative of Christ-in-the-Church to Christ in the whole Christ (i.e., the sick man—'ye visited *me*'). This is there-fore not merely a matter of individual conscience and witness, but a corporate matter. When Mrs Jones, sick in bed is visited by Mrs Brown from the church, the Church is doing something, offering its liturgy. The whole Christ is already identified with the sick woman ('ye visited me') but the Church-in-Mrs Brown is in her word and deed, to declare this and make it plain to the eye of faith.

There is a considerable difference between this type of visit, and one which is a purely private act of good work done by an individual humanitarian. Mrs Brown, who does this visit, comes as representative of the house- or street-church, which is in its turn representative of the parish or local church, and thus of the whole people of God. Her concern demonstrates not only her own personal identification with the sick person, but the conscious acknowledgement by a group of people in her street, representing a community in her neighbourhood, and finally all mankind, that Mrs Jones's predicament is mankind's and God's in Christ. That is, the Church-in-Mrs Brown, in the presence of Mrs Jones utters 'Amen' to the healing and saving work that Christ has done for it and Mrs Jones. By Mrs Brown's action of love to Mrs Jones, the Church-in-Mrs Brown says 'Amen' to Christ's healing and saving work and so becomes what it is—the healing and saving Church. We are reminded of St Augustine,[1] ' "You are the Body of Christ, and severally its members." Since then you are the Body of Christ and his members, it is your mystery that is placed on the Lord's table; it is your mystery that you receive. To words that tell you what you are, you answer "Amen" and in answering subscribe to the statement. For you hear the words, "The Body of Christ" and you answer "Amen". Be therefore members of Christ that your "Amen" may be true.'

Thus, as it is true of the Eucharist that the Body sees its own mystery placed on the Lord's table, so also it is true of the anamnesis of Christ's healing work, when the Body of Christ-Mrs Brown sees its own mystery in front of it in the person of the sick Mrs Jones. It says, by word and deed, 'Amen' to the fact that Christ is there, not now on the Lord's table, but upon the Lord's sick-bed. The Christ who in his Mystical Body is already present in Mrs Jones, is declared present by the work and deed of the Church in Mrs Brown, and the real presence can be received by faith by all who are witnesses. Thus it is

[1] Sermo 272. Quoted by Davies, J. G., in *Members One of Another*, Mowbray, 1958.

that the sick visit of the Christian life is a making and declaring
present of Christ. The result, as in the Gospel healings, is that
some by faith accept him who is presented to them, and others
reject him. They thereby judge themselves to either salvation
or damnation. The Christ, whose presence has been acknowledged and accepted by the 'Amen' of Mrs Brown, is the one
who is Love, who shows God's love. He said 'Even as the Father
hath loved me, I also have loved you: abide ye in my love'
(Jn. 15:9). What happens to the Church, in Mrs Brown and
Mrs Jones and all the witnesses, is that by the obedience in an
act of love-faith the love of God in Christ is made present and
available to be received by faith. As in the Holy Communion
we feed on the spiritual food and have fellowship and love with
God and one another, so here too in doing the sacrament of
healing the Church is fed fellowship and love. We shall later
elaborate on what may be the therapeutic side-effects of the
fellowship and love which now increase around the sick person,
remembering the recent emphasis in psychiatric circles on the
place of therapeutic groups and communities. Similarly, the
theological statement that those who accept by faith that
Christ is present, judge themselves to salvation and others to
damnation, will gain fresh interest when we remember that
what is being declared present to be received is love. Once
again we are reminded of recent psychological theories where
inability to receive love is the key to failure to live, and the
grounds of all neurotic illness.[1] In the light of this, if the Church
has been faithful, then around the sick-bed there will be Christ,
the love of God. That love can be accepted or rejected. Now
is the time of salvation.

We see then that the visitation of the sick is the making
present of Christ by the Church's act of obedience. The sick
visitor, whether he or she be a trained medical worker or not,
comes as representative of the Church, where 'representative'
here carries all its meanings including 'authority', 'power',
'delegate', and 'coinherence' (cf. Heb. *shaliach*). It is an identification of Christ-in-the-Church-in-the-person of the sick visitor
with the sick person and his predicament. What is the content,
in terms of action, of such an identification? In case we should

[1] See e.g., Bowlby, John, *Child Care and the Growth of Love*, Penguin, 1953.

think that it is either only doing good deeds, or only preaching, it is well to recall what Jesus himself said about these identifications of himself with the weak through the administrations of men:

Ye gave me meat.	Adequate nutrition.
Ye gave me drink.	Adequate fluids.
Ye clothed me.	Physiologically satisfactory clothing.
Ye visited me (when sick).	Traditional care for sick.
Ye came unto me (in prison).	Prisoner's aid.
Receive him that I send.	Stating who sent you and
Heareth you heareth me.	that it is Christ himself who is come.

These passages show that the occasions when men and women, by their obedience to Christ's command, realise the promises of Christ to be present, are not ecclesiastical in the narrow sense of the word. They are times not only of preaching and praying, and other wrongly-called 'spiritual' occasions, but when dinners are being brought from next door, blankets and soiled clothing washed and dried, and medicines fetched from the chemist. This may seem obvious as we state it now, but is it not fair to say that the phrase 'When two or three are gathered together in my name there am I in the midst of them' is always thought of ecclesiastically? We all associate it, and quite properly so, with prayer meetings. Equally properly we should associate it with everything done by two or three Christians in the name of Jesus. There is no question of degrees of presence according to the 'spiritual' or 'ecclesiastical' nature of what is done in the 'name' of Jesus. He comes with 'a cup of cold water' as he comes with prayer or celebration of the Holy Communion.

The visitation of the sick is the declaring and making present of the whole Christ. It is indeed a Church occasion, but it is only so by the loving response of the people of God to the sickness situation in their midst. This loving response of the people of God is the love of the fellowship (*koinonia*), which will be manifested in healing and preaching, and manifested in spiritual acts such as the giving of cups of water, injection of penicillin, or construction of hygienic latrines. When these are done in the name of Jesus, and acknowledged so to be done, the people of God, the fellowship (*koinonia*) of love (*agape*), identifies itself with and joins itself to, the sickness situation of the sufferer. Such joining means that the sick man is made one with the fellowship of love, becomes a member of them and they of him. The mystical union of Christ with the sick person is a union of fellowship in love, and what is done by the Church in its response to the sickness situation is to declare and make present the fellowship of love in the union of man with man, and man with Christ.

In the light of passages such as Jn. 13:34f and 17:18–26, we can enlarge our concept of the healing work of the Church as a ministry of the priesthood of the laity, in which the Church joins in the offering of Christ on High by an anamnesis of his healing work, whereby the visitation of the sick is a making present of Christ and a manifestation of his glory. We can enlarge it to include the Johannine insight that what is being made present, what is being manifested, what is being remembered, is the love of God from the foundation of the world. A love of God made flesh, whereby men and God are reconciled in a union of love. The sick visitation is a joining in and a proclaiming of the visitation of love in Christ whereby we were all saved to a new life of union in the love of God. At the sick visitation the local church, to paraphrase St Augustine's words again, sees its own mystery on the sick-bed. What it sees is the mystical union of God's love with Fallen Man. By joining itself to that mystical union the local church receives that mystery. By its act of faith-love, shown in ministering to the sick, in shopping, attending to pressure-points, administering antibiotics, and emptying the bed-pan, in praying for the sick and taking Communion with them, the local church says 'Amen' to what it already is, the union in love, of God and man and man, wrought by Christ.

We come then to the paradoxical fact that the local church, in so far as it is a fellowship of love, becomes so by being what it is in acts of love to the sick and troubled amongst them. The union of love between men and God, already the work of God, must yet be apprehended, accepted, received, by acts of faith-love in which men and women risk themselves by sacrificing themselves, deliberately identifying themselves with the predicament of others.

When we speak of the Church in the local fellowship of love identifying itself with suffering, by acts which are based on the effort to eliminate the suffering of men and women as it presents itself in their need for cups of water, food, medical attention, and human company, paradoxically what is made present by such acts of healing, is he who was perfect faith-love-*suffering*. Men and women in the Church are called to heal the sufferer and the obedient doing of this is the moment of salvation, but what they, and all present, are saved into, is a union with Christ who is perfect faith-love-suffering. This is what some interactionist psychiatry speaks of when, reacting from psychotherapy of technique, it favours a psychotherapy in which the transference is a real live situation in the here and now between analyst and analysand in which both must suffer creatively. The therapy is a matter of 'involvement', 'self-exposure', and the limits of the willingness of those concerned to suffer creatively are the limits of therapy attainable. There is real insight here into the Christian affirmation that fullness of life is a life of self-committal to others from the depth of one's being to the depth of another's being, and that this involves suffering love. Within humanism, however, it still remains a formula for life, a guide to successful living, for which the goals and the motive power are human, and the whole project optional. 'In a non-theistic system' says Fromm,[1] 'there exists no spiritual realm outside man or transcending him. The realm of love, reason, and justice exists as a reality only because, and inasmuch as, man has been able to develop these powers within himself through the powers of evolution. In this view there is no meaning to life except the meaning man himself gives to it: man is utterly alone except as much as he helps another.' We can carry this argument no further here; it is the present controversy between Humanist and Christian Existentialists, and, within Christianity, between the historical and mythological schools. We can only state that the orthodox Christian belief is that God *first* loved and that he sent his Son and that it is through him that we love God and man. Thus the redeemed

[1] *The Art of Loving*, p. 72.

life, the eternal life, of faith-love-suffering, is neither optional for man nor set by his own requirements.

Where shall men and women receive this power of love? Here again the New Testament is clear enough. The love of God and the brethren is the consequence of the work of the Holy Spirit whereby we are incorporated in Christ. The 'making present' of Christ which we have spoken of as if it were the work of the Church in obedience to Christ, when he remembers his saving work, when we give a cup of cold water, is the activity of the Holy Spirit. So Baptism, Holy Communion, and giving a cup of cold water are all occasions when the Church by obedience lays hold of the Lord's promises of communion with men. All these occasions are works of the Holy Spirit, in which men and women declare their union with Christ and receive what they are, a fellowship of love between man and man, and man and God. The increase of love of man for man comes in the sacraments, of which Baptism, Holy Communion, and merciful acts of love-faith are the centre. In Acts of Parliament, social legislation, and welfare arrangements, man may develop and utilise the love which is present in all men, but the talent of love is the gift of God, and the supernatural increase of love is a fruit of the Spirit. It is understood, saluted, and reverenced by man's reason, but not the product of man's reason.

The sick visitation is no isolated action of an isolated individual at a particular moment of time. It is a doing of a memorial of what God did when he visited his people. Thus in the sick visitation the Church offers itself in word and deed with the life of Christ, including his healing work, and the sick man who is visited is confronted by love sent from God to heal and to save. The sick person is joined to the Body of Christ. He is joined to the fellowship of Christ, the fellowship of the Holy Spirit, the fellowship of the Body and Blood, and the fellowship of the Saints.[1] He is joined by the fellowship of love.

This fellowship of love which is to be found in the local church, and which, embracing the suffering of its own members and the sufferings of its own neighbourhood, is to be a thera-

---

[1] These four aspects of 'koinonia' are those described by Davies, J. G., in his study *Members One of Another*, Mowbray, 1958.

peutic community, the means of the real presence of Christ, is not because 'man has been able to develop these powers in himself through the powers of evolution' (Fromm); rather it is found in the local church because man has been able to receive these powers in himself through the power of God. This is the result of the activity of love of the Father to the Son, and the Son's work of love for men in his incarnate life and death. This *koinonia* of men and God is by men's *koinonia* with Christ which is effected by the Holy Spirit in Baptism.

But Baptism is a lifelong sacrament, i.e. it is not an isolated incident with no consequences, rather it is an event which issues in new relationships with God and with Man, and its proleptic effects are progressively actualised through the Eucharist. Indeed the Eucharist is the principal means whereby the koinonia is realised. This is succinctly expressed by St Paul in these words: 'The cup of blessing which we bless, is it not a koinonia of the blood of Christ? The loaf which we break, is it not a koinonia of the body of Christ? Seeing that there is one loaf, we, who are many, are one body: for we all partake [metechomen] of the one loaf' (1 Cor. 10: 16, 17).[1]

Thus the fellowship and love of the local church, which is to be joined to the whole parish by works of fellowship and love, and especially by the visitation of the sick, is to be sustained by regular participation in the love and fellowship of Christ at Holy Communion. At this communion the local church are to receive what they are—fellowship and love—but this fellowship and love of the church group is not to be hugged to itself, for to become Christ is to 'visit' all men with love.

Worship, in its restricted sense, must therefore issue in social activity, i.e. the koinonia of the Body and Blood demand recognition of the koinonia and its claims in every walk of life. It is for this reason that the author of the Epistle of St James can say: pure religion and undefiled before our God and Father is this, to visit the fatherless and widows in their affliction (1:27). This is not a 'heresy of good works', but the inevitable outcome in its horizontal aspect of the vertical koinonia with God.[2]

[1] Davies, J. G., op. cit., p. 21.   [2] Ibid., p. 26.

Finally, before we leave this brief summary of *koinonia*, we must bear in mind Professor Davies's fourth aspect of *koinonia* —the *koinonia* for the Saints. By doing so we shall remind ourselves of the dangers of confusing spiritual fellowship, spiritual love, and spiritual community with psychical fellowship. Too often we think of spiritual as opposed to material, and psychical as opposed to somatic. Nowhere is this more marked than in many concepts of Spiritual Healing. We may thus be tempted to think that the *koinonia* of the local church is something which has little to do with earthly things, and so fail to see how such religiously sounding terms as fellowship and love can be the same as the giving of a cup of water, a hot meal, or a blanket bath. The *koinonia* for the Saints assures us otherwise, for St Paul uses this same word *koinonia* to signify the money collected amongst the Gentile Christians to succour the poorer Jerusalem church.

Professor Davies discusses St Paul's use of the word *koinonia* for this monetary collection to assist the saints in Jerusalem, and shows how it stems from the Hebrew holistic concept of life, so that for the Hebrew, St Paul, money which is for the building up of the *koinonia is* the *koinonia*. In the same way we can say that the 'cup of cold water' which is for the manifestation of the Love of Christ and his redeeming work for men, *is* Christ. It really is, together with the words of compassion and the intention of being Christ, as much a sacrament with due form, matter, and intention as the 'cup of blessing'. It *is* a *koinonia* of the Saints for the saints.

To conclude this discussion of the visitation of the sick in terms of the *koinonia* of the local church, we can do no better than quote a further passage from Professor Davies's study (p. 34).

It will be apparent that according to the New Testament teaching diakonia (service) is an essential part of koinonia. Furthermore the koinonia is an apostolic community, a community charged with a mission which is derived both from Christ and from the Holy Spirit. This mission involves not only the preaching of the Word, but also the witness of the life of the koinonia to the indwelling presence of the redeeming God of Love. Koinonia is therefore mission and mission is koinonia, but so also is diakonia mission. That this is indeed the case will be apparent from a rapid glance at our Lord's own ministry. Modern New Testament scholarship refuses to draw any sharp line between Jesus the Healer and Jesus the preacher; his healing miracles were as much a proclamation of the Gospel as the words that he uttered. But his miracles were directed towards man in his totality, in his corporeality as well as his spirituality, to the whole man in his actual situation. Diakonia has precisely this aim, and is equally a preaching of the Gospel. Hence koinonia, diakonia, and mission are but different aspects of the same reality which is the Church of God sent into the created world to bring it back to its Creator.

Koinonia, visiting the sick and giving a cup of cold water in the remembrance of Christ, and mission, are therefore but different aspects of the same one reality, the Whole Christ.

CHAPTER 10

CORPORATE ASPECTS OF PRAYER, SACRAMENTS, AND HEALING SERVICES FOR THE SICK

WE HAVE SEEN in recent years a resurgence of interest in a positive ministry of healing. This was much needed, for generally speaking the Church's activities around the sick have often appeared to be confined to a ministry of consolation with the absence of any ministry of healing. At the best a vague but unhopeful expectation of some ill-defined benefit might accompany the giving of the sacraments, as if they were a kind of ecclesiastical placebo or tonic. In fact these administrations, like their medical equivalents, perhaps owed their popularity to the relief from the sense of uselessness which came to ministers, with the feeling that they were doing something positive, getting on with something in the face of chronic sickness. At its most positive the Church seemed content to be, together with the library trolley, the floral arrangements, and wireless on the wards, an ancillary morale raiser in hospital and home. In this situation the Church often felt a need for a more positive role. Moreover, it was sharply reminded of its failings in this direction by the challenging, if often dubious, activities of groups like the Christian Scientists.

However, a study of the literature of the last fifty years relating to spiritual healing reveals an almost complete individualism. The sick man, master of his fate and captain of his soul, carries the burden of his own disease. On the one hand he is often assured that there is no truth in the belief that personal sin is related to personal sickness, and on the other hand he is often told that personal faith can bring personal health. The ministry of healing thus becomes largely an exhortation to the sick man to have faith and, committing himself to the Love of God, to receive healing.

The result of excessive individualism has been that even when a positive ministry of healing was envisaged the 'model' was individualistic. The typical example of spiritual healing in the literature of the last fifty years,[1] is that of a chronic case of rheumatoid arthritis. The patient confined to bed, with increasing pain and deformity, after many years of illness and medical treatment, at last turns to God, and putting complete faith in him receives the miracle of healing direct from him. The only intermediary in intercession is Christ, and the only intermediary in God's response is the Holy Spirit acting directly on the physical organism of the intercessor. Whilst this picture was sometimes modified on the side of approach to God, by allowing that others might bring the sick man to the point of making his act of faith, or that others might substitute their prayers of faith for those of the sick man, this was as far as the 'model' was disturbed. Had either Baptism or Holy Communion been thought of as healing services then the corporate aspects of these sacraments, half forgotten though these may have been, would have modified this individualistic 'model'. Communion of the sick was thought of as one thing, and healing services as another. The only sacramental act especially connected with sickness was Unction, which, because it had become Extreme Unction, not only was rarely expected to have any healing results, but was also very individualistic and bore the associations of the extreme privacy of the last moments of life. There was of course also occasional resort to the Laying on of Hands but here too, because the corporate aspect was overlooked, this was rarely connected theologically with the Laying on of Hands at other Church occasions. Confirmation, for example, where the candidate is confirmed by, with, and into the Church, was thought of as quite another matter from healing. To put it harshly, the minister took Holy Communion and, very occasionally, Unction, to the sick, as if it were a thing 'to be carried about'. Even the Book of Common Prayer's instruction that at least two other persons should communicate with the sick man and the curate was very often and very lightly set aside. So too, James's wish that the elders of the church should pray over the sick man was rarely remembered, and then

[1] e.g. Large, J. E., *The Ministry of Healing*, ch. 6, Arthur James, 1959; Swain, L., *Rheumatoid Arthritis*, Guild of Health Pamphlet, London; Weatherhead, L., *Psychology, Religion and Healing*, p. 517.

usually interpreted as a succession of visits of one elder at a time.

The excessive individualism of ecclesiastical services to the sick might have been avoided if there had been closer association between ecclesiastical ministrations and other merciful and loving acts done by Christians to the sick. The fatal division, even at parish level, between work and worship, which should be one *leiturgia*, extended into the ministry to the sick. The visitation of the sick by neighbours to bring food, medicines, and clothing, and to give every sort of physical aid was rarely either visibly or consciously associated with the visitation of the Church in the shape of the minister or the Reserved Sacrament that he carried. The sickness situation of man, and God's response to it, which should have been made, as it was in the Ministry of Jesus, the great acted parable, prophetic symbol, or effective sign of God's work in the world, was largely excluded from the life and preaching of the Church. But because sickness and its last outcome, death, is the situation above all others in which men and women experience their predicament of finitude, meaninglessness and sin, the Church must preach the Gospel here or fail in its mission.

It is no accident that so much of the work and preaching of Jesus was centred in work with the sick. His healing miracles are not only Jewish, Isaianic signs; they are also universal symbols of cosmic predicament and cosmic redemption. Joined with the miracles of feeding, control of sea and storm, and raising from the dead, they are effective signs of the reversal of the fall of all creation depicted in Genesis. That holistic myth, which unites the disobedience of the individual representative man and woman with the fall of all nature, leaves its implications for all else in the Bible, and not least for the healing miracles. The healing of the individual sick man by Christ is no isolated event but the first fruits of the reconciliation of the whole created order. The perfect unity of creation, itself an image of the perfect unity of the Trinity, which was destroyed by man's disobedience, is restored by the reconciling work of Christ, so that in one sense all of Christ's work, incarnation, life, and death, are healing miracles, and thus all Christ's sacraments are healing sacraments, even though some may be particularly appropriate for the sickness situation.

Baptism

This is the first great sacrament of healing. By his baptism the sick man is already a member of the regenerated creation and the healing Church. It is only required that he should of his own free will appropriate the free gifts of healing earned by Christ for him. Because baptism joins man to Christ, man participates both actively and passively in the regenerative and healing work of Christ. He is joined to a therapeutic community in which the members both heal and receive healing. He is admitted as a healer and one in need of being healed.[1] He becomes priest to all creation, organic as well as inorganic, working to harmonise all again in the worship of God and enjoying the benefits of that new harmony. Baptism thus makes all men healers and conservationists and research workers, and inheritors of the benefits of Christ's work done in such men. The baptismal service thus offers an opportunity to the pastor to teach those present of the healing ministry of the Church. Teaching on such an occasion has the advantage that there is little likelihood of strengthening false ideas which isolate the healing life and work of the Church from its other activities. It starts from the beginning of infant life with the preaching that the salvation work of God in Christ is a cosmic act in which there can be no complete separation of man from nature, man from other men, or man's body from his spirit. Baptism lies very close to the healing miracles of Christ, and therefore the Church today can very well teach what is done at baptism by using illustrations from the miracle stories of the Gospels in its baptismal liturgy; but it can only do so adequately, if amongst other things, it bears in mind the corporate aspects of the healing miracles. What is done at baptism is a corporate effective sign, and infant, pastor, and congregation are all representatives. Here we have just one indication of how a

[1] We recall here that in the therapeutic community of Maxwell Jones (*Social Psychiatry; a Study of Therapeutic Communities*, Tavistock, 1952) the distinctive roles of patient and doctor, both passive and active, which were present in 'old-time' hospitals, unite, and each person individually in the therapeutic community corporately becomes a healing—being-healed unity.

rediscovery by the Church of the close relation between the healing miracles and the institution of Baptism by Christ, might enrich the understanding of both. If, as has been suggested in an earlier chapter, it was partly because of their relevance to the early Church's need for authority and illustration of Baptism, that the miracle stories came to occupy such a large proportion of the Gospels, then the Church today would be returning to no mean tradition. The variety of the miracle stories, and of the consequent theology of Baptism, would be a corrective to extreme theologies. Thus, for example, in the matter of the relation of faith to baptism, there is a welcome lack of rigidity in the New Testament accounts. Had a later age invented the healing miracles they would probably have taken care to illustrate their own rigidities, and so produce stories in which, for example, all the healed were adults making a conscious act of faith, or alternatively all were infants brought by believing parents. The theology of Baptism and the theology of the healing ministry of the Church lie very close together and the continual communication between them is essential to the health of both. So, too, is the use of illustrations from healing miracles and from the contemporary medical work of Church and State, in the instruction of parents and God-parents at baptism, and in the enlightenment of the whole congregation. Thus from the very start false compartmentalism between body and spirit, Church and world can be overcome, and a basis provided for a ministry of healing in which skilled medical service, good works, prayers and sacraments enrich each other in one redemptive act of worship. In this connection St Mark's account of the healing of the man sick of the palsy at Capernaum, and St Luke's story of the ten lepers might be particularly helpful.

The general connection between Baptism, effecting the restoration and regeneration of all creation, and the work of medical services in healing and research, which can always be hinted at in Baptism, may be elaborated and made more specific on special occasions. Thus it might be appropriate on occasion, as when conducting a healing service or a Hospital Sunday service, to introduce into it a baptism, particularly if there is an adult person, unbaptised, who is seeking the Laying on of Hands, in hope of healing.

Holy Communion

This is the routine preventive and healing sacrament of the Church, for the maintenance and restoration of health. Perhaps it stands in relation to Unction and Laying on of Hands as preventive medicine does to general practice. The Book of Common Prayer requires the celebrant to say as he delivers the bread, 'The Body of our Lord Jesus Christ which was given for thee, preserve thy *body and soul* unto everlasting life', and only our unconscious dualism overlooks this uncompromising holistic attitude. Just as it is tangible everyday bread and wine that is offered in a spiritual offering, and consecrated but tangible everyday bread and wine that is taken as a spiritual communion, so what is taken is for the spiritual health of both 'body and soul'.

Because Holy Communion is a continual remembrance of Christ's great healing life, death, and resurrection, in which all participating receive the life-giving Spirit, it is a healing service. Because it is a corporate act in which all gathered participate of one loaf, and receive one Spirit, it is the healing service which is particularly appropriate for showing forth the communal aspects of everyday sickness and health. It is here that men and women draw close together to the head of the hygienic and therapeutic community of which they were made a member at their baptism. It is here that by their communion with love they become love by partaking of love. This is well expressed by a consultant psychiatrist, who writes,

> As a Christian I ask myself—should not the Church Fellowship be a therapeutic Community based upon the free-flow of Christian love? Should it not be providing the kind of atmosphere in which people are free to be themselves and to find healing in the redemptive nature of an accepting sacrificial love, the love of God mediated by the membership of the Church?[1]

Holy Communion is therefore offered to us as a prophylactic and healing occasion when our love for one another is refreshed,

[1] Martin, D. V., *The Church as a Therapeutic Community*. Guild of Health Pamphlet, 1958.

so that in Christ we heal one another as we are all healed by our Head. Where there is new love for one another, there the sickening power of envy, hatred, malice, and all uncharitableness, which sustains and regenerates neurotic anxiety, is broken. Thus neurotic anxiety and its concomitant psychosomatic symptoms is attacked in the Holy Communion. Those who gather for it, gather to heal each other in body and soul in communion together with Christ. The sad thing is that the separation between the ecclesiastical and the daily life of those who partake is so wide. Communicants very often cannot even see the relation between their interpersonal physical and spiritual needs on the one hand, and their Holy Communion on the other, let alone start to do something about it outside the church buildings. It is for this reason that of recent years, the Offertory, suspect since the Reformation, has come again into its own. Christians are to learn to bring their liturgy of daily work and life to offer it in the bread and wine. So human life and work are offered visibly in Christ to God and are visibly received back, having become in Christ the means of preservation of body and soul to eternal life. Now of such daily work, and daily life, none is more central than the suffering and healing of men and women in the parish. Therefore the sickness situation must itself be made an offertory that it may be received back as a means of grace and healing. A bold Eucharist will show this forth. We can only throw out a few suggestions. Let the sick of the parish and those near and dear to them, bring the wine to the priest at the Lord's table, that the community in them, and they in Christ, may offer all the pain of mind, body, and soul of the parish. Let the district nurse, the W.V.S. member, the doctor, or anyone known to minister to the same sick people, carry the water, that cup of cold water which symbolises the Real Presence of Christ at deeds of mercy. Let these represent the response of the community to their pain. Let the Sunday School teacher, the prayer leaders, the visitors of the Word of God carry the bread. Let them all receive the elements grouped together around the altar that the local congregation may see their sickness-healing situation made by the work of Christ their salvation situation. Let those who have expressed the desire, and been prepared, stay in front of the altar for the

Laying on of Hands or Unction. Then let the congregation, seeing the clinical event made in Christ a healing event, accept it into their mouths and hearts, permitting the sick and the health workers, especially those who have received Unction or the Laying on of Hands, to bring to them the consecrated bread and wine. Such bold usage of the Holy Communion two or three times a year provides the ideal basis for special healing services. In this way both the tendency to undue individualism in the healing ministry and the temptation to divorce it from the everyday life of the Church or the world may be reduced. Again, in such services, efforts must be made to use illustrations both from the healing miracles of Jesus and from the local practical ministrations to the sick, to help all present at the Holy Communion to understand that in each case there is a doing of the Real Presence of Christ which brings judgment and grace to the body-souls of all who participate.

Holy Communion may thus be not only the central preventive and healing service of the parish, but also the central preventive and healing service of small root family or house groups which have sickness within them. It is not the sick person alone, but the root group with sickness within it which needs to be renewed as a healing community. Thus, whilst necessity may frequently justify the private celebration, every effort should be made to gather round the sick person those who are dear to the patient and those who are near by kin, good neighbouring, or medical service. The practical difficulties are no doubt substantial, but the need is great, for nothing could be nearer to the heart of the New Testament than a vital group of people taking Communion about their representative on the sick bed.

There should be the husband, wife, parent, or child. There should be the neighbour who has been helping out, the district nurse, the home-help, the house-church, and others. Then there will be a visible demonstration of the Mystical Body of the incarnate Lord, the therapeutic Word of God. Not only will men and women receive grace, but by the particular visible means adopted to celebrate Communion they will receive instruction on how to be what they are—the healing Body of Christ.

Holy Unction and the Laying on of Hands

These two practices, well authenticated[1] by Scripture and tradition, are, very properly, regaining their place in the normal ministry of the Church. Unction is no longer associated only with the dying hours but with healing and life. The Laying on of Hands is no longer thought of as an extreme and sometimes dubious practice of a few ministers who feel that they have a special gift, but as a part of every pastor's ministry to his own flock. The corporate aspects of these acts must be considered.

The associations of Laying on of Hands in the Old Testament lie very close to those of anointing. Indeed in the Old Testament the two acts seem to be alternate methods for achieving the same purpose. These purposes included:

(1) Transmission of one person's powers, qualities, and possessions to another.

(2) Transmission of God's powers and qualities to a man.

(3) Transmission by nation or tribe of their corporate powers and qualities to a man.

(4) The election of a man to special position of privilege and responsibility.

(5) The establishment of a permanent relationship between the giver, the intermediary, and the recipient.

(6) The setting aside of a pure sacrifice in an act of cleansing and reparation for sin.

It must be obvious that whatever the later usage of Laying on of Hands and Anointing in the Church's ministry to the sick, and regardless of whether the intended effect is to bring release from sin or healing, or both, the associations of blessing, sacrificing, and commissioning as representatives of God and the people of God must still remain. Therefore Unctions are not just private ceremonies, with the priest as an uninvolved intermediary between God and the sick man, by which blessings of ease of mind and body are transmitted. Certainly blessing and power are transmitted, but at the same time a new

---

[1] See the discussion by Dr C. Harris in *Liturgy and Worship*, S.P.C.K. 1936, and also Dr J. G. Davies in *The Spirit, The Church and the Sacraments*. Faith Press, 1954, pp. 203–11. Also the Report to the Lambeth Conference of 1924 on the Ministry of Healing.

relationship is established between God and God's people, and between his representative and their representative.

The Old Testament associations of blessing, sacrificing and commissioning were not lost by the work of God in Christ. They were fulfilled. Jesus is God's Messiah, his anointed one upon whom God has put his Spirit as he did upon Moses, Aaron, Saul, David, and the suffering servant. So the Synoptists' record of the baptism of Jesus that a voice came down out of Heaven saying 'Thou art my Son, the beloved; in thee I am well pleased', referring to Is. 42:1. But the life and work of Jesus modifies the associations of Laying on of Hands and Unction. The Davidic pomp of the Lord's Anointed, and the worldly splendours of contemporary priesthood are replaced by the kingship and priesthood of the suffering servant. Thus, to be blessed by God in Unction or Laying on of Hands is not only to be filled with power, but to become in Christ a member of the royal priesthood, representative of men, bearing their stripes that they may be healed.

Christ, then, has fulfilled the Old Testament in this respect by a rebirth of the image of the Lord's Anointed upon whom the Spirit of the Lord has rested. Henceforward men must know that there is not only commissioning and blessing to positions of high worldly status, but also to suffering and sacrifice. So too it is with those who receive the Laying on of Hands of Christ and his disciples. There is healing (e.g. Mk. 5:23; 7:32; 16:18; Acts 9:12), Baptising (Mk. 10:16; Acts 8:17–19), and commissioning (Acts 6:6; 13:3). The disciples 'anointed with oil many that were sick and healed them' (Mk. 6:13), but also Jesus is anointed for his burial (Matt. 26:12).

The associations of Laying on of Hands and Unction with the life and work of Jesus and his disciples were therefore such as to widen and deepen the 'typology' of these acts as known to the Old Testament and Judaism. Because Jesus, and later his disciples, manifested a new royal priesthood in which the powers of the new age were present in a glorious wholeness which was yet a suffering servant, Laying on of Hands and Anointing shared in this 'rebirth of images'. Even though early Church practices and later theological definitions might separate anointing with the Spirit by water of baptism from the anointing of the sick,[1] and do so quite properly, they can never do away with their common historical associations, the biblical typology which they share. It is this which resists theological attempts to make too tidy a distinction between the meaning and effects of Baptism, Penance and Unction. The consequence is that whilst we may clearly distinguish Laying on of Hands and Unction from Baptism, Ordination, Penance, or other sacraments or sacramentals, yet we may recognise that they have qualities and effects in common. Thus we may legitimately claim that in Laying on of Hands and Unction for the sick we not only do a remembrance of Christ's effective signs of healing and saving, but we also remember his baptism, his royal priesthood of sacrificial suffering, death, and burial and his resurrection. Thus, those who gather round the sick man do not gather only to do something to the sick man, for by the sacramental act they corporately become Christ as they put on Christ. A new relationship is established between the sufferer, the minister, and the other participant observers of the act and Christ the author of the act, by which all receive Grace. They are all healed as they enter into a new wholeness of a new *koinonia*, and the evil of the sickness, like the evil of the Cross, has been made in Christ the grounds of that fellowship's salvation. The participant observers identify themselves with the sins of the whole world's sickness and sin visibly symbolised in the sick man. They offer themselves, together with the sick man's offering of his own sick self to Christ, and God anoints them and him with his Spirit, giving them power to be little Christs in this sickness situation. Thus, in these acts there is far more than a spiritual counterpart to the administration of a dose of medicine by the physician, though there is such administration. Rather, by these acts and the obedience and faith of the participants, sickness and sin are made to be salvation events. The sickness situation, which threatens all goodness and all meaning is, by the victory of Christ, made to witness to the goodness of all Creation and the meaning of all life.

It is necessary, therefore, in conducting these acts to bear in

---

[1] This is already present in the New Testament for the verb χρίω is used for anointing with the Spirit (Baptism) (Lk. 4:18; Acts 4:27; 10:38; Heb. 1:19), but not of physical anointing. Instead the verb ἀλείφω is used (e.g. Mk. 6:13; Matt. 26:12; Jam. 5:14).

mind the social nature and implications of the act. This does not, of course, mean that there must invariably, or even normally, be many present besides the pastor and the sick man, though there should be frequent enough group and public acts to ensure that this aspect is never overlooked. One practical possibility is to place Laying on of Hands and Unction within the parish communion or within services in which the work of local health services and hospitals is remembered. Not only the sick man but those near and dear to him should on occasion be prepared and blessed together by one or both of these acts. So often in the case of chronic sickness, it is not the patient but another who bears the greatest burden. Disease which incapacitates a wife or husband threatens the marriage and the whole family. It is the whole family who must be obedient to their election to preach the Gospel of Christ by responding in him to the sickness situation which confronts them. They have been elected to a ministry which offers in its life a continual remembrance of Christ's healing and suffering work. The Church through its ministers and local congregations recognises such a calling and after preparation ordains them as their representative. At this point the possibility of elders or other lay representatives actually laying their hands together with the minister's on the sick must be seriously considered. This would not only recover a strand in early Church practice of commissioning and anointing, but would be excellent for portraying the corporate aspect of the sickness-salvation situation.

We cannot discuss here the full meaning of Laying on of Hands and Unction and their general usage. However, it is asserted that such discussion must take seriously the corporate aspects of these acts. One suggestion might be made, however. The Church has here, in Unction and Laying on of Hands, two sacramental acts, and with the recognition that Extreme Unction was a medieval innovation[1] departing from a tradition of Unction as a healing saving act, these two may have become so close as to be confused. Even within one tradition priests vary their indications for Unction extremely widely. In this situation it might well be profitable for the Church to decide

---

[1] For discussion of this, see Dr Harris's contribution to *Liturgy and Worship*, S.P.C.K., 1936.

to reserve Unction for those cases where disease has placed serious burdens, with actual or potential grave and long-standing damage to wholeness, upon individual or group. There is in this distinction a recognition similar to that between a calling to a full-time ministry and a calling to all Christian men and women to witness for Christ in common incidents of everyday life. Where disease in a family means a prolonged burden, then, without in any way suggesting that the disease is not evil, or that it is God's will, it may be said that those who carry that burden are especially called to be God's witnesses in the world by offering it to God that he may make it a salvation situation, in the local community. Personal calling, local calling, and church authorisation make of Unction a service of 'ordering' to a ministry in the sickness situation, which should be as solemn and yet as joyful and full of promise as the form and manner of making, ordaining, and consecrating of bishops, priests, and deacons.

The use of Unction as a service directed to those families who carry a special burden of sickness should be a regular practice of parish life and worship. Its use whilst dictated by the needs of individuals and individual families, should not be casual, but together with prayers for the sick, and sacraments, be built into the parish's plans for preaching the Gospel and doing the Gospel to the sick, for the Unction service is a means of communication and education and committal. By the public service the sick person and his family become known as in need of fellowship and as being willing to offer fellowship. The natural result is that the congregation must follow them out of the Church into the world and into their homes, as an effective sign of the new unity and wholeness of God's work done in the sacrament of Unction. Unction, therefore, like all the healing sacraments, requires preparation not merely of the sick person, but of the people of God, who are to recognise the sick man's calling to be their representative and their responsibility. Plans for Unction include, therefore, not only liturgical plans in the narrow sense of the word, but plans to do a whole *leiturgia* and to offer with Christ an acceptable sacrifice to God about the sick man and his family. Plans and commitments for regular prayers, regular taking of Communion, physical assistance, financial

aid, and medical treatment, are all part of the preparation for
Unction. Willingness to receive such help and admit 'strangers'
into their home—often a stumbling-block—and to accept their
help in prayer, sacraments, and menial tasks, is part of the
preparation of the candidate and his family. The organisational
links between Unction, home-helps, parish Communion, street
church, and the Public Health Department are part of what is
offered for God's anointing. By the unction of his Spirit he will
make of such organisational links a reconciling, healing communion between God and man, and man and man. The annual
or biannual or quarterly event of Unction might be supported
by a monthly event of Communion of the sick, when particular
Christians who have solemnly pledged themselves at the time
of Unction to enter into fellowship with the anointed one and
his family, go with the parish pastor after Communion to carry
their love and service with the Reserved Sacrament to the sick
man and his family. The possibility of permitting certain elders
or specially suitable persons, such as the Christian who made
a special vow at Unction, to distribute the consecrated elements
for this occasion only might be considered. It would permit the
service in the parish church to end with a general dispersal of
parishioners carrying the sacrament to the homes of the chronic
sick.[1]

There is one more of the many other aspects of Unction
which we must mention, and which will come as a natural
introduction to the very difficult problem of the sacrament of
Penance. The Laying on of Hands, so closely associated with
Unction, was used in the priestly cult of Israel. Leviticus
instructs that on the Day of Atonement the priest, representative
of the whole community of Israel, shall take a goat without
blemish and 'lay both his hands upon the head of the live goat,
and confess over him all the iniquities of the children of Israel,
and all their transgressions in all their sins, putting them upon
the head of the goat, and shall send him away by the hand of
a fit man into the wilderness' (Lev. 16:21). This idea of a pure

[1] Dr Harris writes (op. cit., p. 567) 'He [Beza, Calvin's successor] personally
approves the practice, mentioned by Justin Martyr, of sending Eucharist to the
sick by the hands of the deacons, either immediately after the public Eucharist,
or at least on the same day, on the ground that distribution of the elements may
fairly be accounted part of the public service—one and the same action (*una et
eadem actio*) therewith.'

offering as the means of atonement with God has always been important in Christian thinking about the atoning work of Christ. The unspotted offering of an animal on the Day of the Atonement is replaced by the Lord's Anointed, the sinless person who suffers unmerited mental and physical pain in his life, and unmerited penal death. By this act Jesus made of Unction something more than the sum of blessing and commissioning, for he made also of it a reparative sacrifice which produces between God and Man, and thus between man and man, an At-one-ment, a reconciliation into a state of being perfectly loving and perfectly loved. Therefore, in some way dimly understood, Unction in a Christian group of a person who has to carry more than an ordinary share of suffering, which neither he nor they have personally deserved, is participation in the atoning work of Christ. The holy oil on the head is the chrism that makes the sharers of the unmerited suffering of the group, with the anointed one in their midst, into little Christs. 'And there should be no greater comfort to Christian persons, than to be made like unto Christ, by suffering patiently adversities, troubles, and sicknesses. For he himself went not up to joy, but first he suffered pain; he entered not into his Glory before he was crucified.'[1] The innocent[2] suffering situation thus becomes in Unction a remembrance of Christ's unmerited suffering by which men and women enter into a new life. The anointed person is to say with Paul, 'It is now my happiness to suffer for you. This is my way of helping to complete, in my poor human flesh, the full tale of Christ's afflictions still to be endured for the sake of his body which is the Church' (Col. 1:24, N.E.B.). Unction is thus the occasion of a reminder and an acceptance of the fact that suffering in Christ is the greatest creative activity of human life. The redemption of mankind by the sacrifice of the whole incarnate, innocent, suffering life of Christ, which was once done for us is to be remembered in us day by day for the redemption of his whole Body. This is the queer paradox, that whilst the relief of suffering is great, the acceptance of inevitable suffering either in oneself directly or

---

[1] Book of Common Prayer, Order of the Visitation of the Sick.

[2] It is not meant that the sick persons are without sin, but that their sickness is not attributable directly to their sin, and that if they have made confession of their sins, they are suffering as innocents.

by voluntary sharing of another's suffering, either in an attempt
to relieve it or to share the inevitable, can become the greatest
and most creative of all human activities. Unction is at once
the sign of the unmerited death and burial of Christ (Matt.
26:12) and of the promise of the glory of his resurrection.

There is therefore in Unction a sacrificial aspect in which men
and women make of the unmerited suffering in themselves and
in others the occasion of a reparative sacrifice for all men in
Christ. Whilst not being ostentatious, this is nevertheless a
social matter, a corporate effective sign of the unique sacrifice
which is done in front of other people and which offers them
judgment to salvation or damnation. Those doctors and others
who have been privileged to visit men and women who make
of their sickness and death a glorious life, neither something
negative nor something terminal, but a creative force, will know
how much they are judged at such times, becoming aware at
one and the same time of their own pettiness and meanness and
of the possibilities of a fuller, richer life. This is the courage to
be in Christ in the very teeth of existential anxiety due to the
threat of meaninglessness and death.

Penance

It is perhaps significant that we found ourselves above using
a quotation from the Order for the Visitation of the Sick in the
Book of Common Prayer. It seems possible that we are now
getting beyond the stage of mere revulsion against certain
aspects of the Elizabethan concept of the Church's ministry to
the sick, to the stage of attempting to recover much that was
good in it. It seems possible that as the last twenty-five years
have seen a rediscovery within the positive ministry to the sick,
of Laying on of Hands and Unction, the next twenty-five years
may show a renewed interest, within the positive ministry to the
sick, in the place of confession, absolution, and penance, but
that these will only become understood along with an understanding of the corporate nature of wholeness. The successes
of the confessional of psychotherapy, made possible by faith in
the continuing acceptance and absolution of the therapist, is
likely, in combination with the present effort of the Churches
to get back beyond pre-Reformation Church abuses and

Reformation prejudices, to produce fresh sympathy of the non-Roman Churches with the practices of auricular confession, absolution, and penance. There must, of course, always be a revulsion against the idea of God as a hostile Father who rains down sickness on individuals who upset him by their sins. For this reason the Prayer Book Order for the Visitation of the Sick, whatever the authors' original understanding of it, needs drastic revision. Nevertheless there is in Christianity an inalienable connection between sin, suffering, love, sacrifice and redemption in Christ. The rejection of this connection leaves the pastor dumb when visiting the sick. Sickness may or may not have been caused in the individual by distinguishable physical, psychological, or spiritual deficiencies which call for remedy, but it is invariably an occasion on which such possible aetiological factors are to be borne in mind. For example, it is very right and proper in cases of acute dyspepsia to examine one's way of life at all levels, including the nature of the food taken, the nature of one's daily timetable, the nature of one's personal relationships, and indeed one's whole way of life. Thus even a prudent desire to recover from a present illness, or to prevent a recurrence, makes a spiritual self-examination and penitence essential. The leading of a sick individual towards penance in an act of penitence and absolution and reparation is central to the Church's ministry of healing, but because so much psychoneurotic and psychosomatic illness is a symptom of the wrong relations of a group to each other and to God, it is the confession, absolution and reparation of the small group openly to each other, and in the sight of God and the Church, that is powerful for health and wholeness. There is, of course, more involved in the call to penitence, absolution, and reparation at times of sickness than just prudence with regard to future personal health. The Bible always supposes that there might have been something worse than a world in which there is sin with accompanying suffering, and that is a world of sin alone. Just as in medicine there are terrible possibilities in painless illness, such as silent cancers, silent syphilis, silent congenital anaesthesia, silent (because of lack of insight) psychosis, so in the spiritual life silent drift towards spiritual death without the painful chastisement of disappointment, grief, and pain is, from the Bible's point of view, a thing to be dreaded. As a man may be thankful that an attack of pain revealed a hidden complaint and enabled it to be treated before is was too late, and may praise God for 'sending' the pain, and helping him and the doctor to take proper notice and action, so it is that we may feel that sickness is permitted by God. This is surely what the author of Hebrews, quoted in the Visitation of the Sick, means when he writes 'For whom the Lord loveth he chasteneth' (12:6). Certainly even this truth is fraught with difficulties, but many of these spring from the fact that the matter may be looked upon too individualistically. In medicine, one man's pain, by calling early or first attention to sickness in others, may not save him, but others. So it is that the recognition by others of implications for themselves of the sickness of a neighbour offers them possibilities of salvation. Particularly is this so when the sick person by his Christian response has already shown the way to salvation. Thus the sickness situation offers to the group possibilities of penance in an act of forgiveness and reparation. The reparation, it need hardly be said, is not a purchase of a change in God's attitude to us or of our attitude to each other, but the tangible changes in our lives which at once make possible our acceptance of the unchanging love of God and begin the new life in fellowship with God and man. For this reason Penance, a corporate effective sign of a particular form of union of Christ with his whole body, is visibly manifest in *koinonia*. It takes the form of the sick person, and those about him making of the sickness situation an occasion of self-sacrifice. This sacrifice is seen in the quality of the care of the sick person and the quality of his response. Innocent suffering, which once in Christ's saving life and sacrificial suffering was the means of our redemption, is made available here and now through the local church, by the local church voluntarily accepting and joining itself to the suffering which is in its midst. All service to another which causes pain to oneself is innocent suffering. We are reminded again how the therapeutic groups and communities of modern psychiatry identify themselves with the problems and pains of members of the group. They do not merely listen passively, and forgive and accept 'dispassionately'. They commit themselves, they forgive, and accept others 'passionately', and heal not by 'cheap grace' but by 'costly grace'.

We see then that, when the corporate recognition of sickness as a manifestation of a fallen world leads to a corporate response of Penance, in which penitence, reception of forgiveness, and reparation combine in unity of thought and action, there is a healing sacrament of the Church. This in no way implies the acceptance of any general rule as to the relation between individual, or even social, sin and the origin and distribution of disease, but because man's response to disease in his own person, let alone in the lives of others, is never perfect, and usually gravely inadequate, it invariably calls for private and public penance by those who witness it. In this act of Penance, the contrition, the acceptance of God's forgiveness, and the institution of measures to have a saving, healing fellowship with the sick person are part of one and the same act. So, for example, the local church meeting at one and the same time recognises the dire need of elderly people in the parish for a cooked meal, is penitent about its previous neglect, accepts the forgiveness of God, and determines to start a local meals-on-wheels service, by which they may offer their *koinonia* with God and man.

We must conclude this chapter with a reference to the corporate aspect of prayers for the sick. Fortunately this is something which has been widely appreciated of recent years and in very many parishes a serious attempt has been made to pray corporately for the sick. Apart from general prayers for the sick, it is now comparatively common for the minister leading the prayers to mention the names of those who are sick, and where suitable to give some details of the disease and the most troublesome symptoms. It has been discovered that to pray for 'Mrs Jones, who has not slept for four nights because of pain in the chest' is perfectly reverent and provokes more effort at responsive prayer amongst the congregation than general appeals for the sick. With time the practice becomes acceptable, and members of the congregation will ask for their own or loved one's troubles to be put before God in the congregation. Visiting clergy or laity will seek the permission of the sick person to remember him at the local service, and even the stranger or lapsed Christian will commonly accept and make thereby a first public act of faith.

Besides prayers in the whole congregation, special prayer groups are frequently formed to pray for and with the sick. The sick themselves, especially when their sickness brings long hours of enforced physical inactivity, are particularly valuable members of such groups. The success of recently formed fellowships and clubs of men and women sharing the same disease, such as diabetes, epilepsy, and poliomyelitis, demonstrates how valuable for mind, body, and soul such mutual help can be. The helpful activity of completely bed-ridden patients is often reduced to letter-writing and sometimes even to thought, so that they can bring help to each other only by prayer. The establishment and maintenance of such prayer circles amongst the chronic sick is a part of the parish programme to the sick. It must of course be keyed in with the general administrative plan and the communication plan in particular, so that it helps to originate and sustain local groups of active Christians, ten to twenty strong, who feel they belong to each other and the parish. The work of such local groups as originators and sustainers of a community health service at street or neighbourhood level, by co-operation with the local health authority, is discussed in the final chapter.

CHAPTER 11

THE CHURCH AND THE
PSYCHOTHERAPEUTIC GROUP

R. J. CORSINI[1] distinguishes group psychotherapy from other group activities which are not primarily ameliorative, and from larger therapeutic communities of fifty or more persons. He defines group psychotherapy as follows: 'Group psychotherapy consists of processes occurring in formally organised protected groups and calculated to attain rapid amelioration in personality and behaviour of individual members through specified and controlled group interaction.' He then gives a description of the manifold types of group therapy and following this he details the diverse mechanisms which the advocators of these group therapies maintain to be essential to success.

The general atmosphere of such psychotherapeutic groups is difficult to describe except by a lengthy verbatim record such as will be found in books like Dr Corsini's or Dr Foulkes'.[2] To those who have not read such records and have not been present at such a therapeutic group the only description is by analogy. The atmosphere and discussion is similar to that which sometimes is found between acquaintances when under the influence of firelight and evening quietness they surprise each other by speaking openly and deeply of their own relationships and confess to each other what they really think about themselves and each other. In this situation, of course, the therapy is accidental, whereas in group therapy there is a deliberate pursuit of therapy, and to this end a stubborn determination by the members to expose themselves, their problems, and their feelings, to each other. Two things might most surprise an uninformed observer. First, the frankness of the personal exchanges and the heat which is engendered but does not destroy

---

[1] *Methods of Group Psychotherapy*, McGraw Hill, 1957, p. 5.
[2] *Group Psychotherapy*, Penguin, 1957.

the group, seeming rather to be its very source of energy. Second, the interpretation of every word and gesture by members of the group, using the technical terms of the particular theory of motivation held by the group.

The general result is that a member of such a group can confess his deepest feelings and sins to others and find that his problems are understood and that he is not thrown out. He finds, perhaps to his surprise, that he is not the only one with this kind of problem, and that others are interested in him and his problem and want him to overcome it. He finds relief in working off hot feelings which were threatening all the time to break out in undesirable actions, and himself searching his character for explanations of his problems and receiving instruction in this self-encounter, both directly from other members and indirectly by hearing them describe their own ups and downs. He finds father figures, mother figures, brother figures, boss figures and opposite sex figures in the group and learns to live with them in preparation for living with those whom they represent in the outside world. In psycho-drama groups different members of the group act the part of one of their member's family and friends, and stage a typical problem of personal relationships. Corsini sums up the essential ingredients for successful group therapy as follows: 'More generally, in effective group psychotherapy there must be love, understanding, and action. There must be love of fellow men, knowledge of oneself, and good works.'[1]

When we turn to the New Testament we find the nearest equivalent to these general recipes for effective group therapy in the instructions given by the writers of the Epistles as to how the recipients should treat each other. These are of course general rules, and whilst they are sometimes given explicitly they are often only implicit in the discussions and decisions which we find in the New Testament upon particular problems of personal and social ethics. In these latter the particular social, economic, and philosophical structure in which the problems arise involves a 'reality testing' of these general rules, which is as stern and as full of problems as is involved in taking the principles of individual psychotherapy into group psychotherapy and of

[1] Op. cit., p. 48.

group psychotherapy into the wide world. The general principle of *koinonia* had been visibly demonstrated after Pentecost: 'Then they that gladly received his word were baptised . . . and they continued steadfastly in the apostles' doctrine and fellowship, and in breaking of bread, and in prayers. And fear came upon every soul: and many wonders and signs were done by the apostles. And all that believed were together, and had all things common; And sold their possessions and goods, and parted them to all men, as every man had need' (Acts 2:41–45). But from the very beginning Christians belonged to the real world of kingdoms, republics, civil servants, commerce, households, and slavery. So, for example, St Paul, writing in the Epistle to Philemon, to a wealthy man, head of a Christian household, about one of his slaves who has broken the law, has a problem of adopting the rules of fellowship to a wider society. In a similar way the application of the general principles of group psychotherapy to wider society poses delicate problems, of which the present-day clash between some psychiatric and forensic opinion over the treatment of delinquents is indicative. Therefore if we wish to compare the general principles of group psychotherapy as given above with their counterpart in the New Testament we should look at the general instructions for behaviour in the small Christian group, and not at the detailed instruction for relationships between such groups and 'the powers that be', or at instructions for solving particular problems of Church discipline which must have had larger communities in mind.

Let us look at some of the general principles for personal relationships in the early churches. The Apostle James wrote, 'Is one of you ill? He should send for the elders of the congregation to pray over him and anoint him with oil in the name of the Lord. The prayer offered in faith will save the sick man, the Lord will raise him from his bed, and any sins he may have committed will be forgiven.' Then he adds, 'Therefore *confess* your sins to one another, and *pray* for one another, and then you will be healed' (Jam. 5:13, 16; N.E.B.). A small group is here envisaged in which Christian men and women will feel able to speak to their fellows of their sins in the confident expectation of understanding and of a positive concern to help as exemplified by prayer. The cure of souls, 'the rapid amelioration in personality and behaviour of individual members' by other members is commended highly by James, who writes, 'My brothers, if one of your number should stray from the truth and another succeed in *bringing him back*, be sure of this: any man who brings a sinner back from his crooked ways will be rescuing his soul from death and cancelling [A.V., 'hide'] innumerable sins' (Jam. 5:19, 20; N.E.B.).

St John writes, 'We for our part have crossed over from death to life; this we know because we *love* our brothers. The man who does not love is still in the realm of death' (1 Jn. 3:14; N.E.B.). Love is life, hate is death, says the apostle, putting his twentieth-century ideas on group therapy into a nut-shell. St Peter says something similar: 'Above all, keep your *love* for one another at full strength, because love cancels [A.V. 'covers'] innumerable sins' (1 Pet. 4:8; N.E.B.). These words of St James and St Peter ('cancel', 'cover', 'hide') may seem offensive to our modern minds, suggesting a heavenly ledger-book and the treasury of merit, but if we remember that in Hebrew thought a covering for sin is not a legal or market transaction but a sacrificial action we find ourselves close to modern thought. A sacrifice of a pure offering of love shown in concern to help our fellow who has strayed, is effective for healing, for it repairs broken relationships between man, Man and God which were the root of the disorder. Such love brings relief from sickness, whether that sickness be experienced as sin or disease.

Here is another prescription for small group relations, this time from the Pastoral Epistles. 'You must live at peace amongst yourselves. And we would urge you, brothers, to *admonish* the careless, *encourage* the faint-hearted, support the weak, and to *be very patient* with them all. See to it that no one pays back wrong for wrong, but always aim at doing the best that you can for each other and for all men' (1 Thess. 5:14, 15; N.E.B.). Again, St Paul writes, 'If a man should do something wrong, my brothers, on a sudden impulse, you who are endowed with the Spirit must *set him right again very gently*. Look to yourself, each one of you: you may be tempted too. *Help one another to carry these heavy loads*, and in this way you will fulfil the law of Christ' (Gal. 6:1-2; N.E.B.). This text is often quoted when

exhorting Christian men and women to bear each other's burdens of hardship in matters of mind, body, and estate. But the
apostle here is asking us to bear the burdens of another's temptation and sin: our besetting problem such as alcoholism, idle-
ness, frigidity, philandering, or depression is to be shared with
our little group in Christ and become the object of their group
forgiveness, understanding, prayer, and encouragement. Speaking about bitter debates between Christians over the matter of
the propriety of eating meat which could have been sacrificed
to idols, St Paul writes, 'Let us therefore *cease judging one
another*'; but the same Paul, referring to a grave and persistent
scandal in the church at Corinth, says '*Root out the evil-doer from
your community*' (1 Cor. 5:13; N.E.B.). The author of Hebrews
speaks of fellowship as a sacrifice, reminding us of what Peter
and James have said about loving concern 'covering' many sins.
He says, 'Through Jesus, then, let us continually offer up to
God the sacrifice of praise, that is, the tribute of lips which
acknowledge his name, and never forget to *show kindness* and
to share what you have with others; for such are the sacrifices
which God approves' (Heb. 13:15–16; N.E.B.).

These texts have been quoted neither to define exactly what
were the qualities expected of the early Christian group nor to
suggest that expectations were always realised, for we know only
too well that they were not, but they do show something of what
were the principles of Christian fellowship and their resemblance
to the qualities of an effective psychotherapeutic group. The
words in italics above might be used for a satisfactory description of psychotherapeutic groups.

'Love of fellow men, knowledge of oneself, and good works'
(Corsini) are all commended. One of the New Testament
quotations given above may, however, cause concern. The idea
of decisions being taken 'to root the evil doer out of the community' may sound contrary to the general principles of
acceptance, love, forgiveness, and support, but in fact even in
psychiatry such decision is commonly in front of the therapeutic
community and occasionally in front of the smaller therapeutic
group.[1] It is important to emphasise this because some
psychiatrists and laymen whom they have influenced forget

---

[1] Cf. Jones, M., op. cit., p. 42.

that even the highly protected and carefully selected psychotherapeutic group has sometimes to do something about the
patient who will not or cannot stop his attempts to break
up the group. They forget that psychotherapeutic groups who
have learnt 'to cease judging one another' may yet have 'to
root the evil doer from their [your] community'. They seem to
suggest that the Christian fellowship should never make any
minimum requirement for continuing membership and never
make positive moral demands. This problem seems a grave
stumbling-block to some Christians and we must therefore deal
with this at some length.

Most of the many forms of psychotherapy have in common
the disciplined pursuit by the therapist of an accepting or unjudging attitude towards the patient. Indeed, because this is
the only common factor amongst such a diversity of methods,
some psychiatrists confidently assert that all methods are but
earthen vessels holding the treasure of healing, unjudging love.
Typical of these is Professor C. M. Anderson, who writes,

> No matter what the theory, there is one fundamental technique
> which is used by all: the elimination of hostile or morally
> judgmental attitudes against the patient in treatment. No
> matter what the patient says or does, the therapist treats it as a
> fact to the understood rather than one to be judged.[1]

This quotation not only illustrates a common opinion, but also
reveals two erroneous assumptions upon which such opinions
may be based: the assumptions that all 'moral judgments' are
'hostile' and that 'understanding' is distinct from 'passing
judgment'.

Since unjudging concern for the patient is a common factor
in therapeutic techniques it is natural that this factor is put
high when most psychologists explain their mode of action. Here
is an example of a theory of neurosis and psychotherapy draw-
ing upon recent neo-Freudian object relation schools[2] and
Existential schools.[3] In earliest infancy the person, experiencing

---

[1] *Beyond Freud*, p. 245. Peter Owen, New York, 1957. But N.B. p. 250, where the
author introduces moral judgment under the title of 'critical conceptual judgment.'
[2] Cf. Melanie Klein 'Notes on Some Schizoid Mechanisms', *Int. Journal of
Psychoanalysis*, vol. 27 (1946). Fairbain, W. R. D., 'A revised Psychopathology of
the Psychoses and Neuroses', *Int. Journal of Psychoanalysis*, vol. 22 (1941).
[3] Cf. Laing, W., *The Divided Self*, Tavistock, 1960.

a frustration, expresses his rage against the breast, the only object it knows. This infant then fears that its fantasies have (by the powers of magical thought) actually happened and is terrified at the phantasied results. Either the first object, upon which life depends, has been destroyed and the infant knows the horrible possibility of non-existence, or its destructive hostility has been met with hostility. Thus, according to the theory, are the schizoid and depressive types of unconscious habit of thought established. 'I as I really am will destroy what I love. Better to deny existence to that part of me than to affirm it at the risk of non-being.'

Within such a broad theory of neurosis the older Freudian theory fits well, where that part of the person which is denied absorbs genital love and carries its symbols. Where, within such broad theories, the Edenic state is not perfect genital bliss but a perfect suckling situation, neurosis is seen not as a denial of giving and receiving of phallic love, but as a denial of giving and receiving of maternal breast love. In both cases 'loving' is often defined in terms of 'being' or 'living', and vice-versa. Fullness of health then means having 'the courage to be' oneself without fear or favour. You will know when you have become yourself, because then you will be perfect in ability to love and be loved. But what constitutes this situation of perfect love? The answer is that it is a perfect 'being' and 'allowing to be' between two people. Perfect being what? And perfect letting people be what? Loving, of course! Here is a vicious circle. This is often broken by a Freudian myth of perfect uninhibited sexual inter-course before the fall of civilisation, the effective sign of true love and being. Alternatively, the circle is broken by the neo-Freudian myth of the perfect mother-child suckling situation which is the effective sign of true love and being. The Gospel also defines loving in terms of living (being), but the deadlock is broken by the person of Christ, who is both Life and Love. Christ answers both the question 'Courage to be what?' and the question 'What is love?' St John puts it thus: 'My brothers, do not be surprised if the world hates you. We for our part have crossed over from death to life; this we know, because we love our brothers. The man who does not love is still in the realm of death, for everyone who hates his brother is a murderer, and no murderer, as you know, has eternal life within him. It is by this that we know what love is: that Christ laid down his life for us' (1 Jn. 3:13; N.E.B.).

Thus, according to this type of theory, there is from the earliest days of life a fear of being oneself and a consequent denial of parts of one's personality in an attempt to preserve the rest from attack, fears of what would happen if one were to 'be oneself' with another, or let another 'be himself' with one, leads to impoverishment of personality. As years progress, experiences of hostile judgment, especially from parents or parent substitutes, add to the fear of being. Such experiences of hostile judgment are just as damaging if based on a false perception of parental attitude as on a true one.

Now, such early patterns of denial of the self are, according to theory, not accessible to conscious inspection by the neurotic. They are revealed to the therapist by the courage of the patient who lives them again, with the therapist representing, in the strongest sense of the word,[1] the original part object. The therapist, by his technical skill and personal freedom from neurosis, is able to see the patterns of behaviour underlying the patient's behaviour towards him within this transference situation. The therapist can then, if he judges it timely, reveal the interpretation to the patient. The patient is only emboldened to expose himself within the transference situation and made ready to receive the interpretations, in so far as he feels secure that the therapist, and what the therapist represents, will not attack him. The patient will be testing the therapist all the time, and any adverse or hostile judgments will confirm the patient's neurosis and make him strengthen his defences. The therapist accepts the patient as he is, and when the patient accepts acceptance he becomes what he is. The patient (forsaking dead works) responds by faith to the prevenient grace of the therapist, and, accepting acceptance, is made whole.

This kind of psychological explanation, with its claim that healing comes in response to a steady love, which replaces the real or imagined maternal hostility of earliest days, is attractive to many Christians who were repelled by previous theories

---

[1] 'Representation' and 'transference' have much in common with biblical 'anamnesis'. Cf. M. Thurian, *The Eucharistic Memorial*.

where cure came by gratification or sublimation of repressed
genital love. It recalls the love of Christ, who, bearing all the
envy, hatred, and aggression of men, never ceased to love them:
the Christ who could not be destroyed, but came again to love
and to feed all men who only would accept him. The resemblance is true enough and has led some to suggest that the attitude of the psychiatrist to his patient is a full, perfect, and
sufficient demonstration of Christian love, and the express
image of the love of Christ portrayed in the New Testament.
Such suggestions make the Christian uneasy. If it is further
suggested that all condemnation of sin, all passing of judgment,
and all similar activities are harmful to mental health, then the
Christian is seriously perplexed. If, finally, the New Testament
is quoted in support of such an extreme position, the Christian
is frankly sceptical.

Two questions must now be considered. First, is it true that
the patient experiences no moral judgment in his therapy?
Second, is it true that the New Testament portrays the love of
Christ as unjudging?

It must not be assumed that, because a particular method of
psychotherapy is successful, this necessarily verifies the psychological explanation of the success. The history of modern
psychiatry, not to mention older methods of casting out devils,
demonstrates otherwise. For example, in accordance with the
prevalent theory, Freudian technique at one time aimed at a
largely impersonal manipulation of the patient. The therapist,
seated behind and out of sight of the patient, supposed that he
was doing something like his surgical colleague, teasing away
a repressing capsule of mental scar tissue, to release repressed
material and restore normality. Theory aimed at an impersonal
isolation, but clinical experience contradicted the theory, for
it became apparent that the therapist's own person was involved in the process of cure.

It need not follow, then, that because psychiatrists employ
successfully methods which they suppose exclude all moral
judgments, that all moral judgments are in fact excluded. Such
judgments may be there unobserved, or they may, knowingly
or unconsciously, be reintroduced with a new name, such as the
'critical conceptual judgment' of Professor Anderson.

A patient who has psychotherapy will spend several hours at least in close company with the therapist. A full analysis may take several hundred hours. Now, even before the treatment, the therapist has for the patient a social role and status. In the eyes of the patient he is someone called and authorised and trained to make people 'better'. Thus the patient, in so far as he agrees to co-operate, is agreeing to expose himself to someone who makes people 'better'. This role remains, whatever the interior attitude within the therapy. Whatever the therapist's unjudging attitude, whatever his self-disciplined anomism, whatever his metaphysical or ethical views, he does not and cannot contract out of his social role. Whilst the therapist verbally may be at pains never to pass judgment upon the patient, the patient will nevertheless feel that what the therapist is, both personally and in his social role, passes judgment upon him. The unjudging love of the therapist may be experienced by the patient, as judgment and expectation that he will strive to get 'better'.

The more consistent and dedicated the therapist within his social role, the more obvious his concern to confront his patient's problems, and not merely to label them and set them aside, the more strongly the patient may feel the therapist's judgment and expectation. At the very first interview, there will be careful planning of future appointments. Such deliberations symbolise the therapist's strong belief that 'cure' is no arbitrary and temporary whim of patient or society, but something worthy of prolonged effort, skill, and courage. The therapist's consistence within his role resists, by an unchangeable concern, the anxiety and doubt of the patient, even when that takes the form of violent hostility. What the therapist is and does, insists, in Tillich's terms, that it is worth trying 'to be', even if it means facing the threat of 'non-being'. The therapist must say, 'Neither do I condemn thee', but what he is urges the patient to dare to 'Go and sin no more.'

If the therapist were successful in eliminating every verbal moral judgment, the patient would still experience the therapist's concern as judgment, but, in fact, because the exclusion of hostile moral judgment is the exclusion of only a part of moral judgment, psychotherapy is full of verbal moral judgments, for these are necessarily involved in two people 'speaking the truth in love'. The therapist's endeavour to uncover every defensive position is a perpetual moral judgment. There is no self-knowledge without self-judgment, and no giving of self-knowledge to another without judging him. Modern false pre-suppositions have led to psychological theories which mirrored their author's mistaken antithesis between 'critical conceptual judgments' and moral judgments. The biblical view is more correct. God's truth is his holiness. Christ is the 'true light' (Jn. 1:9), 'the truth' (Jn. 14:6), and truth is something to be done, not merely a cerebral decision (Jn. 7:17). When, for example, the therapist and patient come to know the truth about the patient's feelings towards his father, as distinct from false appearance, they are 'doing the truth' (Jn. 7:17). They 'do the truth', because in interpersonal relations the intellectual recognition and the moral courage in which the recognition is made are one act, so that the truth about 'I-thou' is always moral activity. So, too, the truth about the Father is known in the obedience of the Son. It is one person who says, 'I am the way, and the truth, and the life' (Jn. 14:6). The New Testament supports psychiatry in its wish to replace the old legalistic morality, the old covenant, by true knowledge; but it is clearer in its recognition that this means a New Covenant, and it knows the Father by the Son, not the truth by the therapist.

If by moral judgment is meant a hostile attitude, a rejecting and killing process, an excluding from love and favour, then it is quite certain that Christ had no part in it. This is not his mission, 'For God sent not the Son into the world to judge the world; but that the world should be saved through him.' Final judgments are left for the last day. Not Christ, but the world, makes such hostile rejecting judgments, and Christ's sufferings illustrate the nature and effects of such moral judgments. Yet, because he is the true light, what he is, what he says, and what he does brings the divine judgments into the world. Confronted by perfect love, all but a sinless man must judge himself by rejecting it; he will be judged already (Jn. 3:18), and thus in some way be judged by it in the last day (Jn. 12:48).

Christians therefore must be grateful to psychiatrists who insist on a continuing love towards others, a love which never makes hostile judgments. They must learn to examine their own lives for such legalistic rejections, whitened sepulchres which strive to conceal the rottenness within, but they will know that every other kind of judgment is involved in loving and being loved. If it were not so, then God's love in Christ, being perfect, would have been irresistible and forced salvation.

The suggestion that perfect love eradicates moral judgment is no modern suggestion. There were in St Paul's time those who supposed that if love had done away with the old law, they might as well continue in sin 'that grace may abound' (Rom. 6:1f). They, like some psychiatrists today, have rightly rejected the old law, which brought only condemnation and death (Rom. 7:7f), only to replace it, not with Christ, but with Diana of the Ephesians, the many-breasted goddess who requires nothing of men but that they ask for more. This is the false love, the 'egoism à deux' of poor psychiatry and 'how to succeed and get on with people', which Fromm so devastatingly attacks. This poor psychiatry, this poor theology, which seeks wholeness through basking in each other's 'cheap grace', is different from good psychotherapy or good theology, where reconciliation, the love and knowledge of one another, has been 'bought with a price', by 'costly grace'.[1] In psychotherapy each step forward, each resistance abandoned, is achieved when the patient 'sins boldly' in the confidence of the therapist's unchanging love for him. Where the patient offers what he supposes to be relevant material at no cost to anyone, even though the material takes the form of startling confessions, he makes no progress. 'Doing the truth' in psychotherapy requires love *and* moral judgment.

There is, therefore, no essential enmity between the practice of psychotherapeutic groups and the behaviour of small Christian groups; but this is not to say that either their social situation or their aims are identical, and therefore whilst Christians may look to psychotherapeutic groups for enlightenment about the art of Christian living, a slavish copying may be dangerous. The successes of such groups are many, but they have their failures too. Moreover, they deal with highly selected material, and their members are for the most part those who

---

[1] Bonhoeffer's terms. Cf. *The Cost of Discipleship*, S.C.M. Press, 1948.

have not been able to experience Christian pastoral care or have found it unable to help them, so generalisations about the effect of using their methods in society may lead us astray. However, many people who were sick with neurotic problems, besetting sins, and crippling psychosomatic disorders have been healed through group therapy and we must try to learn how it is done.

Men and women meet in such groups with the express intention of helping each other to health of body and mind. The group is more than a collection of the individuals it represents. Joint responsibility is taken in advising an individual as to what he should do next, though there is no insistence that he should do it. There is thus a big shift of power and responsibility, and the hierarchical structure of individual analysis or hospital society is replaced by a democratic structure. The consultant present has trained the members in psycho-dynamics, and may be consulted as expert and *primus inter pares*, but the individual member of the group listens not so much to his opinions as, to use a Quaker term, to 'the feeling of the meeting'. There is a revolution here in the traditional doctor and patient roles as significant as that in the roles for priest and people advocated by the Reformers. In the psychotherapeutic group and the therapeutic community hospital, we have groups of people engaged in the cure of souls, where the role of doctor and patient has been changed, and where the doctor becomes a member of a healing group in which are set diverse gifts, of which his is the minister of the psychiatric word. The laity have come into their own in the modern community mental hospital. Even this is not all, for it must not be supposed that the laity, whether patients, friends, or non-medical staff are expected to exercise responsibility and initiative in hospital social and administrative matters, leaving the healing to the doctors. This is a false conception which is analogous to the false conception of the role of Christian laity in many Churches, where the parochial church council and annual meeting is not expected to concern itself with pastoral matters but to take responsibility for Church structure and non-religious social matters. In the therapeutic community and the psychotherapeutic group the administrative decision, the concern for others' 'souls' and the decisions about social activities are the work therapy which brings healing. In the community mental hospital the ward meeting, where there is discussion not only of general matters such as divorce, unemployment, and war, but of particular matters like the hospital canteen or the use of the ward TV, is part of the treatment. We are reminded of those in the Church today, who extol the parish meeting where practical decisions and the interpersonal conflicts revealed in making them are the grounds of the religious life, and where interpretations are made using the concepts of biblical theology as the concepts of Freudian psycho-dynamics are used in the psychotherapeutic group.[1]

We can also learn from some of the difficulties and failures of psychotherapeutic groups. 'As in real life, or in a purely non-directive régime, the patient has in the group the possibility of rationalising his neurosis.'[2] Sectarianism and pietism is a danger for psychotherapeutic groups which after the first shocks of being open to each other settle down into a comfortable 'we' feeling, certain that they and they only have the 'gnosis' which saves and has saved them to a superior state of life. There is a self-satisfaction and a smugness about some patients, social workers, and physicians who have had experience of psychotherapeutic work, which Christians will recognise from their own unhappy experiences with Christian sects and pietism. 'The more cohesive a therapy group is, which is roughly indexed by the length of participation of the majority of the members, the more actively the members concern themselves with the boundary problems of the group.'[3] The group becomes concerned to control the admission of new members, and may be reluctant to welcome outsiders who might disturb the group. So Sprott, having quoted Homans's principles, 'If the interactions between the members of a group are frequent in the external system, sentiments of liking will grow up between them, and those sentiments will lead in time to further interactions over and above the interaction of the external system', adds significantly, 'Furthermore this liking will be increased if there is disliking of outsiders.'[4] This is a perpetual problem for leaders

[1] Ecclestone, F. A., *The Parish Meeting at Work*, p. 40.
[2] Bach, G. B., *Intensive Group Psychotherapy*, Ronald Press, New York, 1954, p. 295.
[3] Ibid., p. 190.
[4] Homans, G. C., *The Human Group*, Routledge and Kegan Paul, 1951, p. 112.

of mental or religious therapeutic communities; here pastoral theology and group psychiatry might learn from each other. In this task the experiences of the parish meeting and the psychiatric hospital ward meeting may be particularly helpful because they stand half way between the small group and the boundaryless community. Free discussion in these larger groups, which because of their size are likely to contain individual nonconformists or non-conformist groups, is likely to go some way towards keeping the small groups open.

We have earlier stressed the dependence of men and women upon one another, and in this chapter we have stressed the power and healing that is given to members of small groups who commit themselves in faith, hope, and love to each other. We do not wish, however, to add to the indiscriminate enthusiasm for any kind of community action, amounting almost to idolatry, which we sometimes find amongst its supporters today. We conclude therefore with a quotation from Professor Sprott who, whilst expert in the knowledge of human groups, is sensitive to their possibilities not only for good, but for evil. They may force conformity upon individuals contrary to their real needs. Commenting upon experimental work with groups in industry, designed to increase their productivity, he writes:

> What you have to do, in Lewin's terminology, is to 'unfreeze' the existing level by discussion, persuasion, and agreement, and then 'freeze' the new arrangements of forces at a higher level, or at any rate at whatever level approximates to your intentions. A new conformity is established, and, like the old one, carries the individual member with it. As Lewin puts it: 'It is easier to change the ideology and social practice of a small group handled together than of single individuals.' It is this principle that lies behind the success of Alcoholics Anonymous, and has inspired the slogan of the Chicago Arca Project, to the effect that if you want to tackle delinquency you must 'change the streets' in which the delinquents live. It is the same principle which is having such powerful effects in the People's Republic of China.[1]

By his reference to 'freeze' at a higher level, and to Communist China Professor Sprott reminds us that small group work may

[1] Sprott, W. J. H., *Human Groups*, Penguin, 1958, p. 158.

not only 'unfreeze' the human spirit but 'freeze' it at a new level. Fortunately the 'unfreezing' Holy Spirit comes both unbidden and in answer to the Christian group's prayer to 'Stir up, we beseech thee, O Lord, the wills of Thy faithful people.'[1] The local church's ministry to the sick and suffering in its parish borders is one of the Spirit's answers to such prayer. For the Church's ministry to the sick of the parish brings the 'remnant' face to face with men and women right outside their group, to tackle basic human problems, which, thank God, sharply test nice sociological and theological theories. Such work should help to save the closed group from the dangers of 'frozen' pietistic sectarianism.

[1] Book of Common Prayer, Collect for 15th Sunday after Trinity.

CHAPTER 12

THE CHURCHES, VOLUNTARY SOCIAL WELFARE, AND THE STATE

WE BEGAN THIS book with a brief examination of the medical situation today, with particular reference to the part played by the domestic and community background in the prevention, causation, and healing of disease. We showed how greatly we depend upon each other, and what a great part voluntary service from family, friend, and neighbour, contributes to the national effort in healing and welfare. However, it may still be argued that this is a temporary expedient only and that what is being done partially and inefficiently today by voluntary workers will be done completely and efficiently by State and Local Authority in the near future. This opinion was widespread in the years just before and after the institution of the National Health Service in 1948, although the constitution of Regional Hospital Boards, Hospital Management Committees, Local Executive Councils, and Public Health Committees left much scope for voluntary service in administration. Nevertheless despite the work of such committees, despite the repeated declarations of successive Ministers of Health, and despite the recent expansion of 'Friends of Hospital' societies and of fellowships of various types of disability such as spastics, poliomyelitis, epilepsy, and mental backwardness there are many who still hold this view.

In this view Christian social service could only continue to operate with a full health service through Christians finding their Christian vocation within paid work for Local Authority, Hospital Management Committee, Executive Council, or Health Ministry, for whilst for a few years to come there might be some scope for voluntary societies to initiate new welfare services or to maintain controversial ones, the field would become rapidly narrower and soon disappear altogether. The

State by its superior financial resources, planning ability, trained staff and day-to-day efficiency and consistency would eventually replace every voluntary society. This opinion is still widely held and leads in many quarters to a lack of any sense of urgency about finding an efficient and permanent means of combining voluntary and State effort in various fields, and most especially in the small community of every local area. Even those Local Authorities and Hospital Management Committees which welcome voluntary societies and their workers—and they are many—rarely if ever see the necessity for vigorous research and planning to tap the vast resources of community concern which might be available. We believe that the concept of voluntary service as something which will wither away is false, and is not a true reading of the present trend in medicine and sociology. This trend, with gathering strength, favours the fostering of community life as being essential to full health and it sees philanthropy and mutual aid as the keystone of healthy community life. This general trend is likely to favour a permanent solution for domestic welfare problems by co-operation between State and voluntary society. But this solution is also likely to commend itself for entirely logistic reasons, because the numerical size and special nature of domestic welfare is likely to resist complete solution solely by the use of centrally directed skilled workers using specialised equipment. Methods appropriate for those whom the local community could never adequately help through lack of skill and special resources may be less appropriate for replacing services in which domestic skills predominate. As Western man has discovered, the affluent society can remove a good deal of drudgery from house-work, but many hours of work still remain for 'do it yourself'. The extent of the need for self-help in the shape of mutual aid amongst neighbours in a community has recently been demonstrated by a survey of homes in a South Birmingham suburban area. One in four of the households visited—representing three to four thousand households—seemed to the interviewers to be in a situation of need. This was despite the efficient operation by local workers of the services of the Welfare State.[1]

[1] *Responsibility and the Welfare State*, Report of the Birmingham Social Responsibility Project, p. 28.

It is our contention that the sharing of one another's burdens is the necessity and the fruit of a full national health service and of the Christian life. Human nature is such that there can be no full health without the sharing of the burdens of sickness, so that a perfect health service, where training, organisation, and equipment totally remove the need for self-sacrifice is a logical impossibility. In our discussion of 'wholeness' we insisted that he only is whole who is joined to the suffering of others. For this reason the medico-political question whether 'these needs, so essential to the good life, can best be met by co-operative action outside the State service, or by a further extension of them',[1] is as vital to the work of every church and parish minister as it is to the health services and to the democratic way of life. The home-help service, so lowly and unspectacular, may yet be the contemporary growing-point towards or away from a fuller Christian life in this country, and in the health services in particular. If the Christian Church in this country could sponsor, inspire, and substantially staff, a really local domestic welfare service to the sick, it might at one and the same time transform itself and influence the morale of the secular health services for one or two generations.

By the word 'local' in the phrase 'local domestic welfare services' we imply a reasonably small area embracing a population small enough to share many acquaintances through consanguinity, schooling, church, shopping, local politics, and the various clubs that meet in the vicinity. There is at present no local health or welfare service which has its policy decisions, administrations, and execution at this kind of local level. The public health and welfare services are administered by bodies which are called Local Authorities but which are responsible for populations averaging about half a million. Even the nurse entitled the District Nurse serves five to ten thousand people, and she is employed not by a district committee but by the Local Authority. The general practitioner, another 'local' figure, whilst he serves a smaller number, averaging about two thousand, is under contract not to them but to the Executive Council with administrative areas similar to the Local Authority's. He is not totally immune to public opinion, which

---

[1] Fairfield, Letitia, 'Consumers of Welfare', *Frontier*, IV, 3, 1961.

over the years can demonstrate approval or disapproval of his work by increasing or decreasing his list. However, there is no local body which might, for example, decide that an infant welfare clinic would be a great boon and bring this to the notice of the local doctor, let alone offer financial or personal assistance in its institution. The Local Executive Council, which is responsible for the administration of the General Medical Services can hardly spend a penny on providing types of service which are not already nationally available. Like the general population, they are given opportunity to fill in questionnaires for those who make national policy decisions, but like the general public, whose needs and opinions are scrupulously recorded by mass-observation techniques, enabling central decisions to be made in order to supply suitable consumer goods for their welfare, they may despite this still feel that they are puppets.

The Local Authority is in a somewhat better position, having some funds at its own disposal, so that unlike the Executive Councils they can conceive and execute new medical and welfare services and feel pride in their 'local' achievements, but even here the proportion of their available resources coming from the Treasury is increasing yearly and their autonomy thereby threatened. They are in any case not 'local' in the sense of the word mentioned above.

The Regional Hospital Board which plans the hospital services is appointed by the Minister after consultations, many of them private, with other individuals and interested bodies. It is answerable to the Minister. It sometimes appears self-perpetuating and to change only with the death of a member. It may be no less efficient for this, but it is necessarily quite remote from the 'local' community. It has considerable powers, but is kept on an annual allowance by the Minister. The Hospital Management Committees have many members nominated through local committees, but not of course 'local' in the sense in which we are now interested.

The general shaping of the health services and their administration is in the hands of central bodies, and the participation of really local groups is impossible. This is as we would expect, for the scale of the building programmes, the breadth of the planning, and the complexity of the skills which are necessitated by modern medicine makes centralisation inevitable for the provision of such services as surgery, laboratory investigations, radiotherapy, and ambulances. Few will deny this, though many may deplore the problems of communication and depersonalisation which such centralisation brings; and whilst it is true that in several fields of medicine there is talk of a movement out of the hospital into the 'community', very often, if not invariably, the 'community' here means in fact not the local corporate body but the Local Authority. So, for example, the recent Mental Health Act which emphasises 'community' care, in fact puts burdens not upon local communities but upon the Local Authority. They must provide residential 'half-way houses', mental welfare officers and 'follow-up' of discharged hospital patients. It is the Local Authority, which is not necessarily any more the community than the Hospital Management Committee or the Executive Council, which is given new powers and responsibilities and is increasingly involved in home-help services, meals on wheels, handicapped people's clubs, night watchers, laundry services, and old people's homes; but it is questionable whether these are activities which, like the hospital services, require of their very nature large-scale administration, though they may need machinery for their co-ordination.

The Local Authority is thus increasingly involved in domestic welfare activities which are not for the most part directed towards making available services which require professional skill, special equipment, and large-scale capital investment, but are directed to supplying domestic services which are well within the competence of the average man and woman. Cooking, cleaning, washing, shopping, and conversation over a cup of tea have thus become one of the Local Authority's major concerns, but, as we indicated in our first chapter, the number of those needing such services is formidably large and is overtaxing the Local Authority. Moreover, for every one receiving help there are at present ten who receive such help voluntarily from family, friends, and neighbours. It is not surprising, therefore, that many Local Authorities have welcomed the activities of local bodies like the Women's Voluntary Services and the Old People's Councils. One of the most important questions of today is whether such bodies can have a permanent place in the welfare services or whether they are doomed, having once demonstrated a need and a way of meeting it, to be replaced by a nationally or locally financed full-time service.

Neighbourliness, as the name indicates, is not merely a particular kind of relationship between people in which concern and affection and love is exercised but it is a relationship between those who frequently and naturally meet. Neighbourliness operates within a neighbourhood, which provides it with a space-time nexus permitting certain human patterns and habits. The provision of a suitable nexus is therefore part of public health policy. If, for example, housing policy results in the formation of a community which consists solely of old people, then there is no neighbour to mow the lawns and someone has to be appointed to organise it and perhaps even arrange for it to be financed. Again, for example, if young families are by housing policy removed from the grandparents there is a consequent dearth of 'sitters in' and this service has to be organised and may even have to be paid for. The provision of a suitable physical nexus, in terms of good housing and suitable age and cultural distribution is important, but added to this is the initiation and support of community action to deal with its own problems. It becomes vital, therefore, that those men and women in Local Authority who can determine policy should be aware of the possibilities of social group work which has as its aim the amelioration of hardships and injustices by the formation and sustainment of groups in which mutual aid and altruism can co-operate. This is no new departure, for the Friendly Societies were just such adventures and played an honourable part in our recent social history. Was this, as some opinion holds, just an inadequate social response which the Welfare State has rendered permanently redundant, or is it, as we believe, an ideal solution for certain human needs at local levels?

It will not always be easy for those who work in Local Authorities to take this harder route of social group work, of fostering and supporting local groups. For one thing, whilst it is true that there has been in the recent history of Local Authorities much awareness of the need to educate the general population, and this has led to excellent records in health education and citizenship education by Local Authorities, working through their schools and clinics, there has not been the same tradition of the establishment of community association work, though there has sometimes been financial support for it by grant. On the contrary, the State and Local Authority have in many fields replaced in recent years many voluntary groups, and as a result there is a widespread assumption that voluntary societies may initiate welfare services, but only the State or Local Authority can perpetuate them. Moreover, because the immediate gains in terms of efficiency are usually so apparent it is a perennial temptation to replace voluntary effort by state welfare. For example, a recent survey of 'meals on wheels' has shown how inadequate and inefficient are the laudable attempts of voluntary societies in this direction.[1] The Local Authority will have no difficulty in producing better statistics in this or any other field upon which they care to concentrate. However, as specialist welfare personnel multiply in their numbers and variety, and specialist organisations through which they operate keep pace, each efficient in its own field, the question of overall efficiency arises. The woman next door who voluntarily brought in an occasional cooked meal, may be replaced by the W.V.S. or Red Cross meals-on-wheels service, and this in turn replaced by the Local Authority; but perhaps this same woman listened for the knock on the partition wall at night, broke up the coal in the shed and brought a bucketful indoors each morning, fetched the medicine from the chemist, and the pension from the post office, and stopped for a cup of tea and a gossip. The multiplicity of types of social and welfare and medical workers has already produced a reaction in favour of a common training,[2] and a reduction in the number of workers serving one home, but even the present range would be unable to replace the voluntary services of this good neighbour. The possibility of the recipients' still being lonely amongst such a diversity of visitors is apparent.

The Local Authority has an alternative to consider, and that

---

[1] *Meals on Wheels for Old People*, published by National Council for Old People, London, 1961.
[2] Younghusband Report, *Report of the Working Party on Social Workers in the Local Authority, Health and Welfare Service*, H.M.S.O., 1959.

is the vigorous pursuit of good neighbourliness through the establishment and maintenance of philanthropic and mutual aid groups. At this point the glaring need for a really local centre and organisation will become apparent. Only such a centre, in which locally acceptable volunteers, representing diversity of interest and societies, co-operate to merge the good neighbourliness of its people with the skills of the full-time services, can solve the problem.

There is at present no such unit, nothing between numerous individuals and their various voluntary associations and the Local Executive Council, Local Authority, and Hospital Management Committee. We need a new local community health centre unit for each five thousand to ten thousand population in our cities in which a local statutory committee assumes responsibility for the domestic welfare services in their area, and encourages and co-ordinates the voluntary and paid work in the area. Beneath them in every street we need a street welfare warden analogous to the air raid warden, who has some official recognition, training, and out-of-pocket expenses, with a sign outside his house and an 'office' in his front parlour. He or she by experience comes to know who might help whom. He or she becomes the one to whom neighbours turn in distress. He or she is the one whom neighbours expect will approach them for philanthropy and mutual aid. It is he or she who can be called when Mrs Jones weighing fifteen stone is found at night on the floor of the bedroom with a stroke. He knows who to knock up in the street to lift the patient on to the bed, to change the clothes, to provide a waterproof sheet, to find a change of linen, and to volunteer as a night sitter. The general practitioner can consult him, for example, as to the possibility of night sitters, before making a decision as to whether to send the patient to hospital. For it is he, who, through the local community domestic welfare centre and its committee, makes use of the local voluntary and mutual aid societies whose members have undertaken to assist each other domestically as their predecessors did economically.

Such a local domestic welfare service committee would depend for its success on the design of a relationship between the Local Authority and a voluntary but statutory committee, which

would permit proper safeguard of public funds, and yet leave
freedom and responsibility with the committee. The committee
would have a similar relationship with the voluntary societies
which assisted it in its work. The pattern is familiar in this country, ranging from organisations as large as the University
Grants Committees to the Handicapped Persons' clubs. Several
local domestic welfare committees might share a full-time committee secretary, who might hold a joint appointment with them
and the Local Authority. The District Nurse, the Health
Visitor, the Mental Health officer and others, whilst remaining
under the general direction of the Medical Officer of Health
for training and duty rota arrangements, might be under the
day-to-day direction of the 'local' committee.

Such schemes obviously bristle with difficulties. In the short
run it is easier for the Local Authority to 'lay on' these domestic
welfare services, but in the long run it may not only be thwarted
by a lack of funds and a lack of personnel, but also—and this
will be decisive—its long-term socio-medical effects may be
found unacceptable. If medical and sociological opinion favours
the priority of the local community as the responsible agent for
domestic welfare services, then it is likely to be supported by
democratic political theorists and leaders of religious opinion.
The first are likely to feel that local concern for welfare, with
its possible appeal to a generation which is somewhat dis-
illusioned with the present pattern of local political action,
might lead to the enrichment of local political life. The second
are likely to welcome a call to neighbourly love, which is at
the heart of all true religion. The fact that since the war there
have been established in this country two thousand Community
Associations, nine hundred with premises of their own, and
two hundred with full-time wardens, shows that the idea is not
necessarily impracticable.

The part which the local church should play in these local
community domestic welfare services is apparent. Firstly, by
its life and preaching it must call on all men to serve God in
the service of others. Secondly, it can stir up local opinion and
initiate local community action. Thirdly, its members can make
a vital contribution to the manning of these services both in
leadership and rank and file. The local community health

service unit will require a number of local people for part-time remunerated service who have both local knowledge and a strong sense of vocation. Many more will be needed to serve at street level under the knowledge of the street health aid warden. Without the individual Christian conscience, and the corporate conscience of the local Christian church, such schemes will have little chance of success. However, the contribution of members of the Churches can be fruitful only if they and others engaged in voluntary service will, in their turn, be willing to accept some of the disciplines, both technical and ethical, which are part of the way of life of the trained medical worker. Voluntary status does not relieve the good neighbour from learning and using these techniques.

Fortunately there is reason to believe that voluntary helpers today are willing to be trained and accept discipline. The majority of voluntary philanthropic societies nowadays provide training facilities for their workers and expect their workers to take advantage of them. The general public are becoming aware that 'voluntary' and 'untrained' are not necessarily concomitant qualities in welfare work.

In this situation we can welcome the recent concept of the parish pastor as being in part a social group worker who leads by assisting his pastoral charges to become, under the inspiration of the Holy Spirit, friendly societies based upon love and mutual aid. The pastor's ministry to the sick in the parish is then seen not only as his personal visitation to the sick in home and hospital, but also as inspiring his people by word, sacrament, and example to become a Christian Friendly Society in the parish. To this end the minister employs not only the older pastoral skills, strengthened by modern personal counselling techniques, but also the pastoral techniques available from social group work.

The local church will thus be involved on three levels in healing the sick. Firstly, it will be calling upon men and women to see in the full-time health services a means to Christian service which is a continuation of Christ's healing work. Secondly, together with all other good citizens, it will be calling for, initiating, and staffing, local community domestic welfare services. Thirdly, it will establish visible links between prayer, preaching, the sacraments, and visits of concern to the sick, which will be based upon a parish plan. These three levels are administratively distinct, but they are part of one Christian ministry of mercy and healing and it is the Churches' task to show them as such to the eyes of all men. When men and women through the faithful witness of the Church see the clinical event and the administrative act for welfare and healing as the works of Christ, and when they acknowledge them as such and, like the tenth leper, fall on their knees and offer a Eucharist to God for what he has done, then has salvation come upon them.

We need to surround our beds of sickness with faith. We need to surround our death-beds with faith. I believe we need bands of people who are prepared to meet in the Church building or in the homes to pray for those who are sick. We need people who are prepared to go round to visit the sick. We need people who are prepared to be trained to visit the sick and expound the Bible and co-operate in the Laying on of Hands. We need above all to help patients' relations and friends to see their vocation as healers, to see their vocation to surround the sick-bed by faith and prayer and not by hopeless or Stoical sorrow.

The Church is a healing fellowship, and the vocation of the Christian congregation is to build up the right attitude of faith, hope, and charity, so that Christ can heal today. Lord Eustace Percy's words come alive: 'The more the congregation becomes a healing one, the more it realises its vocation to be a healing fellowship, to be the Body of Christ. And the more it will see what healing power Christians have to give to a half-destroyed world.'[1]

[1] Southcott, E. W., *The Parish Comes Alive*, Mowbray, 1956, p. 122.

BIBLIOGRAPHY

(Unless otherwise stated, published in London)

Anderson, C. H., *Beyond Freud*, Peter Owen, New York, 1957.

Argyle, M., *Religious Behaviour*, Routledge and Kegan Paul, 1958.

Bach, G. R., *Intensive Group Psychotherapy*, Ronald Press, New York, 1954.

Balint, M., *The Doctor, His Patient and the Illness*, Pitman, 1957.

Barnett, C. H., *New Testament Essays*, ed. Higgins, A. J. B., Man. Univ. Press, 1959.

Barr, J., *Semantics of Biblical Language*, Oxford, 1961.

Barton, R., *Institutional Neurosis*, Bristol, 1959.

Beausobre, Julia de, *Creative Suffering*, Dacre, 1940.

Bennett, I., *Delinquent and Neurotic Children*, Tavistock, 1960.

Best, E., *One Body in Christ*, S.P.C.K., 1955.

Bonhoeffer, *The Cost of Discipleship*, S.C.M. Press, 1948.

Boulard, F., *An Introduction to Religious Sociology*, Darton, Longman and Todd, 1961.

Bowlby, J., *Child Care and the Growth of Love*, Penguin, 1953.

Brotherton, J. H. F., *et al.*, *Brit. J. Prev. Soc. Med.*, 1957. 11.196.

Buber, M., *I and Thou*, ed. R. McGregor Smith, Edinburgh, 1937.

Caplan, G., *An approach to Community Mental Health*, Tavistock, 1961.

Carse, J., *et al.*, 'A District Mental Health Service', *Lancet*, 1958. 1.59.

Caudill, W. A., *The Psychiatric Hospital as a Small Community*, Harvard Univ. Press, 1958.

Chalke, H. D. and Benjamin, B., 'The Aged in their own Homes', *Lancet*, 21 March 1953.

Chamberlain, V. C., *Adolescence to Maturity*, Penguin, 1960.

Cohen, J., 'Jung', *New Scientist*, 1961. 10.239.

Corsini, R. J., *Methods of Group Psychotherapy*, McGraw Hill, New York, 1957.

Davies, J. G., *The Spirit, the Church, and the Sacraments*, Faith Press, 1954.

— *Members One of Another*, Mowbray, 1958.

Dodd, C. H., *The Parables of the Kingdom*, Hodder and Stoughton, 1936.

— *The Apostolic Preaching and its Developments*, Hodder and Stoughton, 1936.

Eastwood, C., *The Priesthood of all Believers*, Epworth, 1960.

Ecclestone, A., *The Parish Meeting at Work*, S.P.C.K., 1953.

Fairbairn, W. R. D., 'A Revised Psychopathology', *Int. J. Psy. Analysis*. Vol. 22, 1941.

Fairfield, L., *Frontier*, 1961. 4.3.

Finlay, *et al.*, 'Stress and distress in General Practice', *Practitioner*, 1954. Vol. 172; 183.

Flemington, W. F., *The New Testament Doctrine of Baptism*, S.P.C.K., 1948.

Foulkes, S. H. and Anthony, E. J., *Group Psychotherapy*, Penguin, 1957.

Fromm, E., *The Art of Loving*, Allen and Unwin, 1957.

Garlick, P. L., *The Wholeness of Man*, Highway Press, 1960.

Garratt, F. N., *et al.*, 'Institutional Care of the Mentally Ill', *Lancet*, 1958b. 1.682.

Glass, D. V., *Social Mobility in Britain*, Routledge and Kegan Paul, 1951.

Gruenberg, E. M., *Essays in Social Psychiatry*, ed. Leighton, Basic Books, New York, 1957.

Harris, C., *Liturgy and Worship*, S.P.C.K., 1936.

Hazell, K., *Social and Medical Problems of the Elderly*, Hutchinson, 1960.

Hazelton, R., *Providence*, S.C.M. Press, 1958.

Hendry, G. S., *The Gospel of the Incarnation*, S.C.M. Press, 1959.

Hobson, and Pemberton, 'The Health of the Elderly at Home', *B.M.J.* 1956. 1.587.

Hodgson, L., *The Doctrine of the Trinity*, Nisbet, 1943.

Homans, G. C., *The Human Group*, Routledge and Kegan Paul, 1951.

Hooker, M., *Jesus and Servant*, S.P.C.K., 1952.

Jacob, E., *Theology of the Old Testament*, Hodder and Stoughton, 1958.

Jeremias, J., *The Parables of Jesus*, S.C.M. Press, 1954.

Jones, M., *Social Psychiatry; a Study of Therapeutic Communities*, Tavistock, 1952.

Judge, E. A., *The Social Pattern of Christian Groups in the First Century*, Tyndale Press, 1960.

Kendall, E. L., *A Living Sacrifice*, S.C.M. Press, 1960.

Kessel, W. I. N., *Brit. J. Prev. Soc. Med.*, 1960. 20.

Kilpatrick, G. B., *The Origins of the Gospel according to St Matthew*, O.U.P., 1950.

Klein, M., 'Notes on Some Schizoid Mechanisms', *Int. J. Psy. Anal.*, 1946. 27.

Knight, G. A. F., *A Christian Theology of the Old Testament*, S.C.M. Press, 1959.

Kutner, B., *et al.*, *Five Hundred Over Sixty*, Russell Sage Foundation, New York, 1956.

Laing, W., *The Divided Self*, Tavistock, 1960.

Lambe, T. A., 'Neuropsychiatric observations in Nigeria', *B.M.J.*, 1956. 2.1389.

Lambourne, R., *Frontier*, Summer 1960.

Lampe, G. W. H., *Reconciliation in Christ*, Longmans, Green, 1956.

Large, J. E., *The Ministry of Healing*, Arthur James, 1959.

Leeming, B., *Principles of Sacramental Theology*, Longmans, Green, 1956.

Lightfoot, R. H., *St. John's Gospel*, ed. Evans, C. F., O.U.P., 1956.

Loeb, C., *Textbook of Medicine*, Saunders, Philadelphia, 1955.

Manson, T. W., *Ministry and Priesthood, Christ's and Ours*, Epworth Press, 1958.

— *A Companion to the Bible*, Clark, 1939.

Martin, D. V., *The Church as a Therapeutic Community*, Guild of Health, 1958.

— *Experiment in Psychiatry*. Bruno Cassirer, Oxford, 1962.

Mascall, E. L., *Christ, the Christian, and the Church*, Longmans, Green, 1946.

Mersch, E., *The Whole Christ*, Dobson, 1956.

Mess, H. A., *Voluntary Social Service and the State*, Kegan Paul, 1948.

Mestitz, P., 'A series of 1,817 patients seen in a Casualty Department', *B.M.J.*, 1957. 2.1108.

Milligan, F. S., *Int. Rev. Community Development*, 1960. 5.

Moberly, R. C., *Atonement and Personality*, Murray, 1901.

Mozley, J. K., *The Impassibility of God*, O.U.P., 1926.

Neill, S., *A Genuinely Human Existence*, Constable, 1960.

North, C. R., *The Suffering Servant in Deutero-Isaiah*, O.U.P., 1948.

Pederson, J., *Israel: its Life and Cultures*. O.U.P., 1926.

P.E.P., *Family Needs and the Social Services*, Allen and Unwin, 1961.

Phythian-Adams, W. J., *The Call of Israel*, O.U.P., 1954.

Quick, O. C., *Doctrines of the Creed*, Nisbet, 1940.

Raven, C. E., *New Scientist*, 5 June, 1958.

Rees, J. R., *Amer. J. Psych.*, December 1958.

Report *To the 1920 Lambeth Conference on the Ministry of Healing*, S.P.C.K., 1924.

— *The Family in Contemporary Society*, S.P.C.K., 1958.

— *Voluntary Societies and the State*, Nat. C. Soc. Services, 1952.

— *Meals on Wheels*, National Council for Old People, 1961.

Report *Royal Commission on the Law relating to Mental Illness*, H.M.S.O., 1957.
— *Responsibility in the Welfare State*, Birmingham Council of Christian Churches, 1961.
Richardson, A., *The Miracle Stories of the Gospels*, S.C.M. Press, 1941.
— *An introduction to New Testament Theology*, S.C.M. Press, 1958.
Robins, H. C., *A Guide to Spiritual Healing*, Mowbray, 1953.
Robinson, J. A. T., *The Body*, S.C.M. Press, 1957.
Robinson, W., *Religious Ideas of the Old Testament*, Duckworth, 1936.
— *Inspiration and Revelation in the Old Testament*, O.U.P., 1946.
Rooff, M., *Voluntary Societies and Social Policy*, Routledge and Kegan Paul, 1957.
Shands, A. R., *The Liturgical Movement and the Local Church*, S.C.M. Press, 1959.
Shedd, R. P., *Man in Community*, Epworth, 1958.
Sheldon, J. H., *B.M.J.*, 1950. 1.950.
Southcott, E. W., *The Parish Comes Alive*, Mowbray, 1956.
Spence, J., in *Social Group Work* ed. Kuenstler, P., Faber, 1955.
Sprott, W. J. H., *Human Groups*, Penguin, 1958.
Stafford-Clark, D., *Psychiatry Today*, Penguin, 1958.
Stocks, P., *Studies of Medicine and Population*, H.M.S.O., 1949.
Streeter, B. H., *The Four Gospels*, Macmillan, 1930.
Swain, L., *Rheumatoid Arthritis*, Guild of Health, Undated.
Taylor, V., *The Life and Ministry of Jesus*, Macmillan, 1954.
Thompson, R. H. T., *The Church's Understanding of Itself*, S.C.M. Press, 1957.
Thomson, A. P., 'Reflections on Medical Practice', *B.M.J.*, 19 July 1958. 11.120.
— 'Problems of ageing and chronic sick', *B.M.J.*, 1949. 11.243 and 500.
— *et al. Care of the Ageing Sick and the Chronic Sick*, Livingstone, Edinburgh, 1951.
Thornton, L., *The Common Life in the Body of Christ*, Dacre Press, 1941.
Thornton, M., *Pastoral Theology: on Reorientation*, S.P.C.K., 1958.
— *Essays in Pastoral Reconstruction*, S.P.C.K., 1960.
Thurian, M., *The Eucharistic Memorial*, Lutterworth, 1960.
Tillich, P., *The Courage to Be*, Nisbet, 1952.
Torrance, T., *Royal Priesthood*, Oliver and Boyd, Edinburgh, 1955.
Townsend, P., *Family Life of Old People*, Routledge and Kegan Paul, 1957.
Vriezen, T. C., *An outline of Old Testament Theology*, Blackwell, 1958.

Weatherhead, L. D., *Psychology, Religion and Healing*, Hodder and Stoughton, 1952.

Williams, C., *The Descent of the Dove*, Faber, 1950.

Williams, G., *Voluntary Social Service Since 1918*, Hodder and Stoughton, 1952.

Willmott, P. and Young, *Family and Kinship in East London*, Routledge and Kegan Paul, 1957.

— *Family and Class in a London Suburb*, Routledge and Kegan Paul, 1960.

World Health Organisation, *The Community Mental Hospital*, W.H.O., Geneva, 1955.

Wright, G. E., *God Who Acts*, S.C.M. Press, 1952.

Younghusband, *Report of the Working Party on Social Workers*, H.M.S.O., 1959.

BIBLIOGRAPHY: INDEX OF TITLES

Books and Reports

Adolescence to Maturity, V. C. Chamberlain
Apostolic Preaching and its Developments, C. H. Dodd
Approach to Community Mental Health, G. Caplan
Art of Loving, E. Fromm
Atonement and Personality, R. C. Moberly
Beyond Freud, C. H. Anderson
Body, The, J. A. T. Robinson
Call of Israel, W. J. Phythian-Adams
Care of the Ageing Sick and the Chronic Sick, et al., A. P. Thomson
Child Care and the Growth of Love, J. Bowlby
Christ, the Christian, and the Church, E. L. Mascall
Christian Theology of the Old Testament, G. A. F. Knight
Church as a Therapeutic Community, D. V. Martin
Church's Understanding of Itself, R. M. T. Thompson
Common Life in the Body of Christ, L. Thornton
Community Mental Hospital, World Health Organisation
Companion to the Bible, T. W. Manson
Cost of Discipleship, Bonhoeffer
Courage to Be, P. Tillich
Creative Suffering, Julia de Beausobre
Delinquent and Neurotic Children, I. Bennett
Descent of the Dove, C. Williams
Divided Self, W. Laing
Doctor, His Patient and the Illness, M. Balint
Doctrine of the Trinity, L. Hodgson
Doctrines of the Creed, O. C. Quick
Essays in Pastoral Reconstruction, M. Thornton
Essays in Special Psychiatry, E. M. Gruenberg
Eucharistic Memorial, M. Thurian
Experiment in Psychiatry, D. V. Martin
Family and Class in a London Suburb, P. Willmott
Family and Kinship in East London, P. Willmott and Young
Family in Contemporary Society, S.P.C.K. report, 1958
Family Life of Old People, T. Townsend
Family Needs and the Social Services, P.E.P.

Five Hundred over Sixty, B. Kutner, *et al.*
Four Gospels, B. H. Streeter
Genuinely Human Existence, S. Neill
God Who Acts, G. E. Wright
Gospel of the Incarnation, G. S. Hendry
Group Psychotherapy, S. H. Foulkes and E. J. Anthony
Guide to Spiritual Healing, H. C. Robins
Human Group, G. C. Homans
Human Groups, W. J. H. Sprott
I and Thou, M. Buber, ed. R. Macgregor Smith
Impassibility of God, J. K. Mozley
Inspiration and Revelation in the Old Testament, W. Robinson
Institutional Neurosis, R. Barton
Intensive Group Psychotherapy, G. R. Bach
Introduction to New Testament Theology, A. Richardson
Introduction to Religious Sociology, F. Boulard
Israel, J. Pederson
Jesus and Servant, M. Hooker
Law Relating to Mental Illness, Royal Commission Report, 1957
Life and Ministry of Jesus, V. Taylor
Liturgical Movement and the Local Church, A. R. Shands
Liturgy and Worship, C. Harris
Living Sacrifice, E. L. Kendall
Man in Community, R. P. Shedd
Meals on Wheels, National Council for Old People report, 1961
Members One of Another, J. G. Davies
Methods of Group Psychotherapy, R. J. Corsini
Ministry and Priesthood, Christ's and Ours, T. W. Manson
Ministry of Healing, J. E. Large
Ministry of Healing, report to the 1920 Lambeth Conference
Miracle Stories of the Gospels, A. Richardson
New Testament Doctrine of Baptism, W. E. Flemington
New Testament Essays, C. H. Barnett, ed. Higgins
One Body in Christ, E. Best
Origins of the Gospel according to St. Matthew, G. B. Kilpatrick
Outline of Old Testament Theology, T. C. Vriezen
Parables of Jesus, J. Jeremias
Parables of the Kingdom, C. H. Dodd
Parish Comes Alive, E. W. Southcott
Parish Meeting at Work, A. Ecclestone
Pastoral Theology: on Reorientation, M. Thornton
Priesthood of all Believers, C. Eastwood

Principles of Sacramental Theology, B. Leeming
Providence, R. Hazelton
Psychiatric Hospital as a Small Community, W. A. Caudill
Psychology, Religion and Healing, L. D. Weatherhead
Psychiatry Today, D. Stafford-Clark
Reconciliation in Christ, G. W. H. Lampe
Religious Behaviour, M. Argyle
Religious Ideas of the Old Testament, W. Robinson
Responsibility in the Welfare State, Birmingham Council of Christian
    Churches
Rheumatoid Arthritis, M. Swain
Royal Priesthood, T. Torrance
St. John's Gospel, R. H. Lightfoot, ed. Evans
Semantics of Biblical Language, J. Barr
Social and Medical Problems of the Elderly, K. Hazell
Social Group Work, J. Spence, ed. Kuenstler
Social Mobility in Britain, D. V. Glass
Social Pattern of Christian Groups in the First Century, E. A. Judge
Social Psychiatry: a Study of Therapeutic Communities, M. Jones
Spirit, the Church and the Sacraments, J. G. Davies
Studies of Medicine and Population, P. Stocks
Suffering Servant in Deutero-Isaiah, C. R. North
Textbook of Medicine, C. Loeb
Theology of the Old Testament, E. Jacob
Voluntary Social Service and the State, H. A. Mess
Voluntary Social Service since 1918, G. Williams
Voluntary Societies and Social Policy, M. Rooff
Voluntary Societies and the State, National Council of Social Services
Whole Christ, E. Mersch
Wholeness of Man, P. L. Garlick
Working Party on Social Workers, Report, Younghusband.

Articles

'The Aged in their own Homes', H. D. Chalke and B. Benjamin,
    Lancet, 21 March, 1953
'A District Mental Health Service', J. Carse, *et al.*, *Lancet*, 1958,
    1.59.
'The Health of the Elderly at Home', Hobson and Pemberton,
    B.M.J., 1956, 1.587
'Institutional Care of the Mentally Ill', F. N. Garratt, *Lancet*, 1958,
    1.682
'Jung', J. Cohen, *New Scientist*, 1961, 10.239.

'Neuropsychiatric observations in Nigeria', T. A. Lambe, *B.M.J.*, 1956, 2.1389

'Notes on Some Schizoid Mechanisms', M. Klein, *Int. J. Psy. Anal.*, 1946, 27

'Problems of ageing and the chronic sick', A. P. Thomson, *B.M.J.*, 19 July, 1958, 11.243 and 800.

'Reflections on Medical Practice', A. P. Thomson, *B.M.J.*, 19 July, 1958, 11.120

'A Revised Psychopathology', W. R. D. Fairbairn, *Int. J. Psy. Anal.*, Vol. 22, 1941

'A series of 1,817 patients seen in a Casualty Dept.', P. Mestitz, *B.M.J.*, 1957, 2.1108

'Stress and Distress in General Practice', Finlay, *et al.*, *Practitioner*, 1954, Vol. 172, 183.

Amer. J. Psych., December 1958, J. R. Rees

B.M.J., 1950, J. H. Sheldon

Brit. J. Prev. Soc. Med., 1957, 11.196, H. J. F. Brotherton

Brit. J. Prev. Soc. Med., 1960, 20, W. I. N. Kessel

Frontier, 1961, 4.3, L. Fairfield

Frontier, Summer 1960, R. Lambourne

Int. Rev. Community Development, F. S. Milligan, 1960, 5

New Scientist, C. E. Raven, 5 June 1958